POND LIFE

written by

Richard Manuel

illustrated by
Chris Shields

COLLINS
London and Glasgow

First published 1991
© in the text Richard Manuel 1991
© in the illustrations Chris Shields 1991
ISBN 0 00 458825 8

Chris Shields thanks
National Museums and Galleries on Merseyside
for the loan of specimens

Colour reproduction by RCS Graphics, Leeds
Printed and bound by
Wm Collins Sons and Co Ltd, Glasgow
1 3 5 7 9 10 8 6 4 2 0

Contents

Introduction   4

Ponds and pond life   8

  Threats to ponds   8

  Types of pond life   9

  Water plants   10

  Water animals   11

  The pond year   11

  Looking for pond life   18

  Collecting pond life   20

Life above the water   22

The water surface   109

Underwater life   116

Terms used for plant leaves   234

Index   235

Introduction

This book is an introduction to life in ponds: not only the underwater world but also the fringe of marginal plants and the associated animals that are so characteristic of ponds. Water is such a congenial environment that it supports many more life forms than can live on land, including numerous organisms so minute that they can only be seen with a microscope. We only include those that you are likely to be able to see with the unaided eye – though a simple magnifying glass will be useful for a closer look at some of them.

A pond has been defined as a body of standing (that is, not constantly flowing) water, shallow enough over its whole extent to allow the growth of rooted aquatic plants. That description includes nearly all stillwaters in the area this book covers, including many of those

called lakes. In the British Isles only the vast, deep glacial lakes of the Lake District of England and the Welsh mountains, the Scottish lochs, some of the Irish loughs and a few modern lowland reservoirs fall outside this definition. Even in these the shallow margins have much of the quality of ponds. In this book *pond* is used to indicate any small stillwater (less than a stone's throw across) whereas a larger pond will, quite arbitrarily, be called a lake.

The region covered

The variety of plant and animal life in various geographical and climatic regions differs widely. The species here are limited to those found in western Europe, an area of temperate conditions. This includes the whole of the British Isles and extends into continental Europe to the Loire Valley in the south-west, the German Democratic Republic and Poland in the east, bounded by the mountainous regions of the Alps in the south and Scandinavia in the north. Most species will be generally distributed throughout this area but some are more local. When a distribution is described as 'southern' this means that it will be found within an area roughly formed by the southern half of England and Ireland plus areas south-west of the Rhine. The 'continent' refers to Europe excluding Britain.

Within this area there is a major difference between upland and lowland locations. Typical lowland ponds are nutrient-rich, usually with hard/alkaline water, and are often a little warmer. Upland waters are often (but not necessarily) nutrient-poor, with soft/acidic water, and their altitude usually makes them cooler. In upland areas of alkaline rock, where the soil and hence the water is richer, ponds are uncommon features due to the porosity of the rock.

NOTE: *To save unnecessary repetition, and because they are most abundant, all descriptions refer to inhabitants of rich lowland ponds, unless specifically stated to be upland pond or acid water species.*

Arrangement of species

The book is divided into three main sections: above the water, the water surface and underwater. Plants and animals are placed in the section where you are most likely to see them. Some animals, voles for instance, dive beneath the water but you will see them more clearly above it and they are therefore in that section. Others, such as dragonflies, spend part of their life cycle underwater, part above – you will find them twice, each stage in the appropriate section.

Plants are themselves often divided into above- and underwater parts and they have been described according to where the most noticeable part of the plant appears.

Names

'Common' names have been used when they exist but not all organisms have one. A plant or animal may also be known by several different names and the same names may be used for different things – sedge, for instance, is both an insect and a grass. Scientific names, which are always given, following the common names if they exist, are understood universally. Do not be put off because they are in a form of Latin – gardeners use them all the time, often without realising it (*Primula, Iris* and so on)! They consist of two words printed in *italics*, the first always has a capital letter and is the *genus* (plural *genera*), a group of closely linked species; the second (no capital) is the *species*, the plant or animal itself. For instance, the duck genus *Anas* contains several species, such as *A. penelope* (Wigeon) and *A. crecca* (Teal). When only the initial letter of the genus is given this means it is the same as the last genus mentioned. In some cases organisms are so alike that only the *genus* will be given.

A group of related genera form a *family* – the duck genus *Anas* (together with *Aythya* and others) belonging to the Duck family, Anatidae. Families are used here when appropriate to make the book easier to use but are not always included.

Measurements

All measurements are given in metric units: millimetres (mm), centimetres (cm = 10 mm) or metres (m = 100cm); weights are in grams (gm) or kilograms (kg = 1000gm). Lengths apply to bodies only and do not include legs, tails, antennae or other appendages. As a rough guide to those who still prefer imperial measure 1cm = 0.4 in, 1m = 39 in, 1kg = 2.2 lbs. A multiplication sign (✕) by an illustration indicates magnification greater than life size.

Ponds and pondlife

Few ponds are truly natural, nearly all are man made. The natural succession (by gradual encroachment of plant-life) from open water to marsh or fen, and eventually to dry land, takes only a few hundred years if nature is left to take its course, so any natural pond is relatively short-lived.

Man-made ponds include 'village-green' and 'dew' ponds, originally constructed for watering live-stock; stewponds for raising table fish, or nowadays also for angling, and landscaped, purely ornamental waters. Others are by-products of human activities: quarrying, gravel extraction, peat digging and civil engineering works, even bomb craters. Excavations for railway embankments left numerous long, narrow, trackside ponds, and canals are long narrow ponds with occasional water flow. The few natural ponds are such as ox-bow lakes by river courses, fen or bog pools, naturally eroded spring pools and mountain tarns.

The presence of a pond can often be sensed long before it is seen. Changes in the vegetation, an increase in insect life, birds swooping after insects and other such signs all signal 'here is water'.

Threats to ponds

Ponds are under increasing pressure from pollution, land-fill schemes, agriculture and development. In the writer's own neighbourhood there are now less than half the ponds there were 25 years ago. Conservation organisations are working to halt or even reverse this sad situation. Please help by *never* throwing rubbish into ponds, trampling banks, picking flowers or digging up plants. If you are an angler do not leave discarded tackle, especially fishing line, weights or other debris behind. Animals have been ensnared in line and poisoned by lead weights. Ponds can be beautiful, peaceful places but are easily spoiled by the selfish acts of a small minority. Respect these fragile environments and help preserve them for the future.

Types of pond life

A pond is a rich environment supporting not only submerged (aquatic) organisms but a whole gradient of habitats – submerged, emergent (with wet feet), marginal and so forth – relating to the water and its surrounds. Plants fit neatly into such categories whereas animals may, at different stages of their lives, occupy different habitats.

Ponds attract all kinds of life from large birds like the heron to the smallest microscopic organisms. Some will be familiar, others you may not even recognise as being plants or animals. Generally people have no difficulty in telling an animal from a plant but some of the simpler animals, such as sponges and hydras, do superficially resemble plants. While most water plants are obviously plants, with green leaves, roots and flowers, some of the specialised floating ones look quite different and lack most of these features. Algae are simple plants forming both plant-like and unplantlike shapes – but beware of confusing them with sponges or some protozoans that also form shapeless green masses.

Water plants

Water plants range from the truly *aquatic* plants, which grow submerged in the water, although their flower stems may emerge, to waterside plants which only rarely get even their 'feet' wet. In between, on the pond edges (or margins), comes a wide variety of rooted or free-floating *emergent* plants with either submerged, floating or *aerial* (emergent) leaves – sometimes two or three types on one plant. Many are not fussy about whether they are in water or not, as long as they are near it. Also included in the bankside fringe may be various land plants which are not reliant on being close to water: they just happen to be there. Examples of these are nettles, willow-herbs, docks and dandelions; there is no space to include them in this book and you should consult more general wild flower guides.

When trying to identify a plant the shape of the leaves is a most useful feature. Many marginal plants are grasses or have slender grass-like leaves, others are 'broad-leaved'. Terms used in this book to describe leaves and their arrangement are explained on page 234. The structure of the *inflorescence* – the whole flower stem with flowers or, later, seed heads is also important.

Water animals

The larger animals are the most familiar – birds, mammals, frogs, newts etc. These are all animals possessing backbones (*vertebrates*). All others, lacking a backbone, are *invertebrates*: these include relatively familiar creatures such as snails, worms and insects, and also many other types which can only live in water and hence are less well known.

Life underwater differs greatly from living in air. To obtain oxygen some animals breathe air through the surface, others use the oxygen dissolved in water, absorbing it directly through their skins (effective only in very small creatures) or by special structures called gills. Gills vary widely in appearance in different animals but basically function by drawing water over an absorbent surface which may be platelike or finely divided to increase its surface area.

As on land, there are carnivores (which eat other animals) and herbivores (plant eaters) but additionally many animals feed on detritus (sifting through mud or debris for edible matter) or are filter feeders. The latter typically use their gill mechanisms to filter tiny creatures or particles of organic material from suspension in the water. Unlike air, water is full of such material. Detritus and filter feeders are nearly all invertebrates.

The pond year

Seasonal changes affect pond life profoundly. A pond in winter shows little evidence of the abundance of life that swarms at warmer times. The cold of winter

11

and much reduced light levels effectively halt plant growth. Most plants, including the vital plant micro-organisms at the base of the food pyramid, die back until spring. During winter they exist as spores, seeds or buried roots or tubers, although some submerged plants make special winter-buds that remain dormant until bursting into growth in the spring.

Cold and the lack of plants for food slows the growth of animals too. Many cannot function at all at near-freezing temperatures. Some survive through winter by hibernation; others form over-wintering bodies of various types: sponges make gemmules, water fleas ephippia, and many mites, insects and worms exist only as eggs or inert pupae, the adults dying off at the onset of winter.

In spring the lengthening, warmer days trigger a reawakening. Fresh green shoots appear on many plants, catkins and buds on the willows. Birds, generally inconspicuous in the winter (apart from winter-visiting ducks) start courting and nest building. Amphibians return to water to prepare for breeding; frogs may already have spawned in a mild February or early March. Eggs, pupae and other

over-wintering stages of invertebrates start to hatch. As the light levels and temperature increase, the water gradually becomes alive with myriad wriggling, hopping, swimming tiny creatures. The sudden availability of food enables fishes to fatten after the lean winter and to get fit for breeding later on.

By June the crescendo of life has reached its peak. Plants are grown and flowering. Trees are in full leaf, providing shade from the sun's full power. Birds are kept busy throughout the long days providing food for their insatiable rapidly growing young. Tadpoles are swarming and blackening the pond's edges, if they have not already grown legs and left the water. Many fishes have spawned, or soon will, their fry wandering in aimless shoals, providing a plentiful food supply for the young of many predators which bred earlier. The invertebrate life has become amazingly rich: water fleas of many kinds abound, often clouding the water and yielding another food resource. Many of the insect larvae and nymphs are maturing and emerging from their aquatic childhood into winged adults. Bankside foliage conceals many of these during the day, the evening bringing the greatest insect activity: mayfies pursue their brief

Pond in spring

nuptial flights, sedgeflies are skittering across the surface, reluctant to use their newfound powers of flight, and buzzing swarms of midges hover over the margins, their numbers apparently undiminished by the diving attacks of swallows and martins.

This wondrous array of life continues through to early September, some species declining in numbers as others take their place. Eventually the shortening days and increasing night chills make their occurrence felt. Many of the flowering plants have withered, reeds and rushes lose more leaves than they gain. Soon the trees will donate their leaves to the rich bottom compost of the pond. Swallows and other birds gather in migration flocks. Occasional battered dragonflies still hunt the few surviving other insects – mayflies and sedges having a final fling. Underwater, the numbers are dropping rapidly: water fleas are becoming scarce, as are the insect larvae and mites that prey on them. The great larder of fish fry is nearly empty and the survivors by now larger, quicker and wiser. As on land, the creatures of the pond are pulling down the shutters on another year, bracing themselves for the rigours of winter and anticipating the joys of next spring.

Looking for pond life

Whilst many of the larger animals and plants can scarcely be overlooked, the multitude of tiny creatures that live in or around a pond must be searched for deliberately. At first many will be missed, but with practice the necessary skills will be acquired.

Life above the surface can be studied *in situ* with little more than a keen pair of eyes, aided by a magnifying glass for small species or binoculars for distant ones. Do not forget that most animals are easily scared by a heavy footfall or a shadow cast suddenly across them.

Simply looking into water, provided it is reasonably clear and calm, can be very informative. Kneeling at the water's edge you can see a suprising number of creatures. Further away from the bank the view is often obscured by ripples or glare reflected from the surface – polarizing sunglasses are good for reducing this effect.

When searching for small animals, remember that most avoid direct sunlight. The underside of stones or lily leaves are good places to inspect, but remember to replace them as they were. Sunken twigs and

19

branches which have been submerged for some time are often encrusted with a fine variety of living things, as are the older (darker) aquatic roots of willow and alder. If you have a net it can be worked carefully through dense plant beds, or just skim the mud surface. The tinier creatures thus captured can be studied as described below. If you are lucky enough to catch a fish or newt remember not to handle it with dry hands or you will damage the delicate waterproof skin, and, as with the rest of your catch, put it back once you have admired it.

Collecting pondlife

Sooner or later the inquisitive pond addict will want to study pondlife more closely than is possible by just looking into the water. The easiest and most efficient method of taking samples is to use a net. Any net is better than none, but the relatively cheap ones sold by pet shops for harrassing goldfish have wire frames that bend too easily. A rigid metal frame, up to 25cm across and firmly fixed to a handle at least 1m long, is best. Ideally the meshes should be 1-3mm apart and made of as strong a material as possible. Fine meshes clog easily, although a fine-meshed net from the pet shop has its uses for sifting out water fleas and similar small creatures.

A netful of debris and small creatures is most easily sorted out in a white dish – anything will do but a plastic tray is especially good. Delicate aquatic creatures need careful handling and a variety of utensils will help in this: spoons, tea strainers, pipettes (droppers) with rubber bulbs, and forceps (tweezers). A magnifying glass will be needed for small creatures which can be individually studied by putting them, in pond water, into any small transparent container. The identification features given in this book for small organisms are designed for use in such conditions.

If you wish to carry a few animals home for further study, or to stock an aquarium, use a clean plastic bucket with a lid. Remember that many water animals are carnivores. Fierce individuals which are likely to gobble up your other samples should be isolated – a plastic bag within the bucket is fine. Remember that pond animals need to be kept *cool*. Do not leave the bucket in the sun or any other warm place, such as a car parked in the sun, or its inhabitants will suffer a slow and unpleasant death. Stick, also, to the following rules:

Do not dig up plants (it is against the law).

Do not transfer specimens from one pond to another (always replace them in the pond they came from). Undesirable species, including disease organisms, are too easily spread in this way and it is never a good thing to introduce species that are not already present. It is against the law to move fishes from one water to another and certain amphibians – Crested newts and Natterjack toads are also protected by law.

A few animals will not survive in captivity. Sponges in particular will not only die quickly but their rapid decomposition will soon foul the water and kill everything else.

21

Life above the water

The following section describes those plants and animals which are somehow tied to the water but do not actually live *in* it: although the plants may grow with their feet in water their stems and leaves are largely dry. Insects are the dominant animals in numbers, because so many have aquatic young stages and their power of flight enables them to travel over water with ease. Many birds are also characteristic of waterside because it is here that they feed and usually breed. Any bird or mammal may turn up at the waterside for a drink or bath but in this book there is only space to describe the specialists.

1

PLANTS

WATERSIDE TREES

Many trees can be found growing by water but only two genera are constantly associated with this habitat.

Alder *Alnus glutinosus* (**1**) can be a shrub or a proper tree up to about 15m tall. Its leaves (**4**) are rounded and prominently serrated. Male flowers (**2**) are firm scaly catkins, borne in small clusters; female flowers (**3**) are green cones, which ripen to brown with a woody texture and last through the winter.

Willows *Salix* range from creeping shrubs to large trees (**1**). Their leaves are oval to lanceolate, usually with serrated edges. The flowers are catkins (males usually yellow, females green ripening to fluffy white, with trees usually only bearing one sex) or 'pussy willow'. Larger willows are often pollarded – the branches cut back – producing characteristic club-shaped trunks with a spray of slender branches radiating from the crown. The timber is of limited value but is ideal for cricket bats, walking sticks etc.

Sallow, Goat Willow or **Pussy Willow** *S. caprea* has more rounded leaves (**4**) than others, dark green above, grey below. **White Willow** *S. alba* is largest (up to 20m) and probably most common and familiar, with soft green lanceolate leaves (**3**), silky grey beneath. **Crack Willow** *S. fragilis* has slightly darker leaves and brittle shoots that snap cleanly rather than bend.

1

Osiers *S. viminalis* and others are smaller plants with very narrow unserrated leaves (**2**). They have for centuries been managed to produce long flexible branches used to make baskets and fencing; beds of these tall shrubs still occur in some marshy areas.

Hybrids are frequent where different species grow together and can cause confusion but the graceful **Weeping Willow** (a hybrid known as *S. x chrysocoma*) is well known and unmistakable.

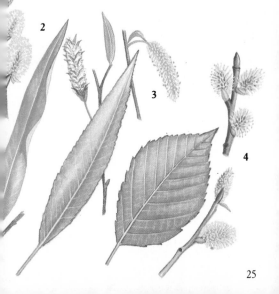

1

2

3

4

26

REEDS AND GRASSES

Grasses are true flowering plants. Their tiny flowers are never colourful but the inflorescence nevertheless forms an attractive display with a variety of shapes and patterns.

Common or **Norfolk Reed** *Phragmites australis* (**1**) is a familiar grass with 3m or longer cane-like stems and broad (2cm or more) stem leaves; the old stems persist through the winter. The inflorescence is dense and brush-like with long soft hairs. This is a common plant which spreads rapidly in shallow water, forming dense beds which can rapidly fill a small pond.

Reed Canary Grass *Phalaris arundinacea* (**2**), common in margins and wet places, is similar to (1) but slightly smaller, up to 2m tall, with rough-edged leaves up to 18mm wide which last throughout winter in a dead, dry state. The inflorescence consists of many dense, separate clusters.

Reed Sweet-grass *Glyceria maximum* (**3**), is one of the commonest plants of bankside and marginal fringes, growing erect (up to 2m) or sprawling along the surface beyond the margin proper. It has pale green stems, long pointed leaves and a densely branched inflorescence.

Floating Sweet-grass *G. fluitans* (**4**) sprawls or floats at pond margins, sometimes forming a floating mat. It is smaller, slenderer and darker than (3), often grey-green, with a sparser inflorescence.

BULRUSH AND REEDMACE

Bulrush or **Common Club-rush** *Schoenoplectus lacustris* (**3**) has submerged or floating strap-like leaves and a leafless stem, up to 3m tall, crowned with a branching inflorescence with clusters of cone-like *spikelets*. It forms beds *in* the water, usually deeper than other marginal plants.

Reedmace *Typha latifolia* (**2**), often wrongly called Bulrush, is a stout plant up to 3m tall with flat, stiff, grey-green leaves about 2cm wide. The female flowers form a fuzzy brown sausage with the yellowish male part immediately above.

Lesser Reedmace *T. angustifolia* (**1**), a much less common species, has a more slender flower head with a gap between the male and female parts and narrow (5mm) leaves.

SEDGES

True Sedges *Carex* are coarse grass-like plants common in pond margins and wet places. The genus includes numerous species that are often difficult to identify. The main aquatic species share a similar growth habit and have stiff V- or M-section leaves. The inflorescence consists of several dense spikes, often on stalks, with female spikes below and differently formed male ones above, on strongly three-sided stems. The leaves usually remain green through much of the winter, turning brown and dying back when new growth starts in spring.

Greater and **Lesser Pond Sedges** *Carex riparia* and *C. acutiformis* are both about 1-1.5m tall, with grey-green M-section leaves and scarcely-stalked spikes. Greater (**1**) has brownish male spikes and leaves up to 15mm wide; Lesser (**2**) has purplish male flowers and 6-10mm wide leaves.

Cyperus Sedge *C. pseudocyperus* (**4**) has pale green leaves and long-stalked pendent spikes, females greenish, the solitary male slender and brown.

Bottle Sedge *C. rostrata* (**3**) has narrower (7mm) greyish leaves and slender, stalkless, drooping female spikes. **Water Sedge** *C. aquatilis* (**5**) has V-section leaves 4-6mm wide, greyish above but bright green underneath, and erect spikes. This and (**3**) occur mainly in upland regions.

Great Tussock Sedge *C. paniculata* (**6**) forms unmistakable massive raised tussocks, up to 2.5m tall, in marshes and wet places.

Great Fen Sedge *Cladium mariscus* (**3**) forms graceful tussocks of long, slender, three-sided and harshly serrated grey-green leaves. The 2m tall stems bear numerous stalked flower clusters. Rather local in areas of extensive fen, such as the Norfolk Broads, it is uncommon elsewhere but often introduced as an ornamental plant.

Spike Rushes *Eleocharis* are distinctive sedges with erect stems arising in rows or clusters, and no proper leaves. The flowers form a single cone-like spike at the top of the stem (barren stems pointed). **Common Spike Rush** *E. palustris* (**1**) has cylindrical stems up to 75cm tall. It grows in shallow water or marshy places, often forming beds. **Needle Spike Rush** *E. acicularis* is smaller and very slender, with (usually) four-sided stems. It often grows submerged in deeper water, especially where the level drops in summer, allowing it to flower when dry.

Cotton Grasses *Eriophorum* are sedge-like plants with distinctive white tufted cottony flower heads. *E. angustifolium* (**2**) is the Common species, up to 75cm tall, with several flower tufts per stem. It grows in bogs and marshes, especially in acid upland areas. This grass is readily noticed and identified at a distance and, as it often grows *over* quaking bogs or deep marshes, its presence indicates that the walker should proceed with caution.

1

2

3

33

TRUE RUSHES

True Rushes *Juncus* include numerous species, many of which grow in wet or damp places. The few included here are widespread, typically waterside plants, occasionally found growing in shallow water, but there are many other possible species and accurate identification requires a specialist guide. Rushes form clumps or tussocks of stiff, usually cylindrical stems with the flowers forming a lateral tuft, sometimes several, overhung by a pointed leaf-like bract.

Soft Rush *J. effusus* (**3**) is up to 1.5m tall, the stem smooth or slightly grooved, mid green, and its central pithy core, seen when it is split open, is solid and without hollow chambers (**3a**). Compact Rush *J. conglomeratus* is similar but has a ridged stem and is confined to acidic sites.

Hard Rush *J. inflexus* (**2**) is tougher and darker than (1) with a markedly grooved stem whose core is divided into hollow chambers (**2a**).

Bulbous Rush *J. bulbosus* (**1**) is shorter than the others, rarely more than 30cm high, with rosettes of hollow flattish leaves, bulbous at the base. Flower stems are branched with numerous separate flower-heads (which may be replaced by plantlets). It grows with a sprawling habit in marshes or by acidic ponds.

35

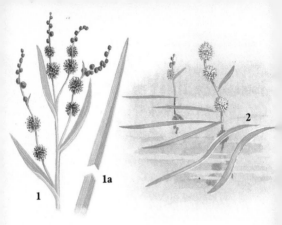

BURR-REEDS

Burr-reeds *Sparganium* are easily identified when the spikey spherical flower clusters are present; otherwise the foliage merges with the grasses and other slender-leaved marginal or submerged plants.

Branched Burr-reed *S. erectum* (**1**) is very common in the marginal fringe. It has stiff, erect, shallowly three-sided leaves (**1a**) up to 2m tall, and a branched inflorescence.

Unbranched Burr-reed *S. emersum* (**2**) has narrower strap-like, keeled leaves that float along the surface and an unbranched flower stalk. It grows in deeper water than (**1**) to about 1m depth.

IRIS AND FLOWERING RUSH

Yellow Iris *Iris pseudacorus* (**3**) is a familar plant often grown in gardens, but also common in most damp habitats and shallow margins. Its greyish, flat and sword-like leaves are up to 2.5m tall, 6cm wide and arranged in a flat fan. The flamboyant yellow flowers are unmistakable.

Flowering Rush *Butomus umbellatus* (**4**) is an uncommon marginal plant with sword-like, three-angled, often twisted leaves. Its pink flowers, about 2.5cm across, form an uneven cluster atop a 1–1.5m stem.

1

WATER PLANTAINS, ARROWHEAD AND WATER SOLDIER

Common Water-plantain *Alisma plantago-aquaticum* (**1**) is a large plant, up to 2m tall, common in shallow margins. Its leaves are oval with prominent veins and emerge from the water on a long erect stalk. The tall, much-branched flowering stems bear many small pale lilac, three-petalled flowers. **Narrow-leaved Water-plantain** *A. lanceolatum* has smaller, narrower leaves and is much less common.

Arrowhead *Sagittaria sagittifolia* (**2**) is another bulky plant, typically occurring in deeper water than *Alisma*. Its leaves grade from strap-like submerged *or* floating ones to the characteristic arrowhead-shaped

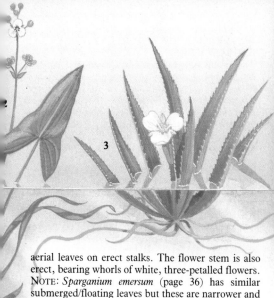

aerial leaves on erect stalks. The flower stem is also erect, bearing whorls of white, three-petalled flowers. NOTE: *Sparganium emersum* (page 36) has similar submerged/floating leaves but these are narrower and keeled.

Water Soldier *Stratiotes aloides* (**3**) is a curious plant, local and uncommon. It forms distinctive rosettes of stiff, pointed, spiny-edged leaves up to 40cm long, green or reddish, with free wiry roots. It sits on the bottom most of the time but rises to break the surface when flowering. The white flowers are three-petalled, each on a modest stalk.

WATER PARSNIPS AND RELATIVES (UMBELLIFERS)

This group includes the Wild Carrots and Parsleys and is characterised by the arrangement of its tiny flowers (always white in aquatic forms) in flat-topped clusters called *umbels* (**1a**). Most are tall, robust, bushy plants but some aquatic species have a creeping or sprawling habit. BEWARE! Many are **poisonous**, one potentially deadly. Those on this page all have once-pinnate leaves.

Fool's Water-cress *Apium nodiflorum* (**1**) sprawls in shallow water, with erect leaves which have up to 12 leaflets with serrated edges (distinguishing them from real Water-cress, page 48). The flowers form tiny stalkless umbels. Fortunately for fools, this species is not poisonous. The similar but feebler **Lesser Marshwort** *A. inundatum* has three-lobed leaflets on erect leaves and finely divided submerged leaves.

Lesser Water-parsnip *Berula erecta* (**2**, *shown to smaller scale*) – also, with *Apium*, known as Water-celery – may grow erect or creeping, often partly submerged. Its long-stalked, erect leaves, with up to 20 lateral leaflets, are strongly toothed, the final one three-lobed, and the small flower umbels have short stalks.

Greater Water-parsnip *Sium latifolium* (**3**) is tall, up to 2m, and robust with large umbels. Its leaves have up to 12 long serrated leaflets plus a simple one at the tip.

Water-dropworts *Oenanthe* are umbellifers with leaves twice (or more) pinnate, and stout, hollow, ridged stems. Their much-divided aerial leaves are more or less deeply toothed and submerged leaves are usually finely divided.

Common or **Fine-leaved Water-dropwort** *O. aquatica* (**3**) grows in water, emergent or sumberged. All its leaves are thrice-pinnate, the submerged ones (if present) with threadlike leaflets. The umbels are short-stalked with pure white flowers.

River Water-dropwort *O. fluviatilis* (**2**), despite its name, often grows in ponds, but needs clean, clear alkaline water. It usually grows completely submerged, forming a bushy growth which quickly spreads to form a dense bed in water up to half a metre deep. Aerial leaves, if present, are twice-pinnate with deeply toothed leaflets. Submerged leaves are similar but more elongated and pointed.

Hemlock Water-dropwort *O. crocata* (**1**), common in southern and western Britain, is a bushy bankside plant up to 1.5m tall, which is **very poisonous**. Its twice- or thrice-pinnate aerial leaves have broad three-lobed, toothed leaflets and the flowers form creamy, long-stalked umbels up to about 12cm across.

TALL WATERSIDE FLOWERS
(Typically 0.5–1m tall)

Purple Loosestrife *Lythrum salicaria* (**4**) bears a magnificent erect spike of starry, six-petalled flowers arranged in whorls, from June to August. The downy leaves are in pairs or threes up the stem, each being stalkless and lanceolate.

Yellow Loosestrife *Lysimachia vulgaris* (**3**), despite its name not related to (4), displays its striking yellow five-petalled flowers on short stalks arising from the leaf axils from June to September. The almost stalkless, oval-lanceolate leaves are in whorls of two to four. Both this and (1) are often grown as garden plants.

Marsh Woundwort *Stachys palustris* (**2**) has a bristly stem and serrated, stalkless, lanceolate leaves in pairs. The blueish-pink, large-lipped flowers are produced in whorls from the leaf axils from July to September.

Gipsywort *Lycopus europaeus* (**1**) is deceptively nettle-like and consequently overlooked or avoided, although very common, especially amongst reeds and grasses just above water level. The tiny whitish flowers (June–September), arranged in dense whorls, are almost hidden in the axils of the deeply toothed, rich green, paired leaves.

1

2

3

4

45

SPRAWLING OR ERECT WATERSIDE FLOWERS

Water Speedwells *Veronica* all have flowers with four unequal petals (**5**) on stalks arising from the axils and serrated leaves. They typically grow on mud or in shallow margins, spreading out over the water.

Brooklime *V. beccabunga* (**2**) is the most common. It has a fleshy, often reddish stem, slightly stalked oval leaves and rich blue flowers. **Blue Water Speedwell** *V. anagallis-aquatica* (**4**) has unstalked lanceolate leaves and pale blue flowers. **Pink Water Speedwell** *V. catenata* (**5**) is similar, but for the colour of its

flowers, and **Marsh Speedwell** *V. scutellata* (**6**) has very slender leaves and white or pale blue flowers, often with darker lines.

Water Forget-me-not *Myosotis scorpioides* (**3**) is a well-known blue-flowered marginal plant distinguished from *Veronica* by its five equal petals and entire, downy leaves.

Water Mint *Mentha aquatica* (**1**) is often found with (**3**) but is usually taller. Its leaves are pointed-oval, hairy, toothed and in opposite pairs. The tiny bluish-purple flowers form tight spherical clusters. A strong minty aroma is often noticed even before the plant is seen.

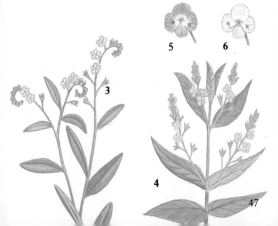

CRESSES, DOCKS AND BISTORTS

Great Yellow-cress *Rorippa amphibium* (**1**) bears spikes of small four-petalled flowers. Its leaves are variable in shape but typically lanceolate with irregular and deep teeth.

Water Cress *Rorippa nasturtium-aquaticum* (**4**) is normally found in clear rivers but turns up occasionally in spring ponds. Its once-pinnate leaves are smooth edged and tiny four-petalled flowers are borne on short erect stalks.

Great Water Dock *Rumex hydrolapathum* (**2**) truly is 'great': 2m tall with massive lower leaves up to 1m long and sprays of numerous tiny red flowers.

Amphibious Bistort *Polygonum amphibium* (**5**) grows in or out of water, erect or trailing along the surface. The green or reddish leaves are lanceolate with short stalks and the tiny deep pink flowers form a dense erect spike.

Water Pepper *P. hydropiper* (**3**) is similar to (4) but the leaves are stalkless and the drooping flower stalk has sparse green/pink flowers. The whole plant has a hot peppery taste.

49

BUTTERCUPS

Lesser Spearwort *Ranunculus flammula* (**1**) is a common plant of damp meadows and waterside muds, where it may become submerged during high water levels. It has erect spear-shaped leaves and yellow five-petalled flowers 5–10mm across.

Celery-leaved Buttercup *R. sceleratus* (**2**) lives in similar places to (1) or in shallow water. It differs in its large three-lobed, deeply toothed leaves with simpler ones above, and small (5–7mm) yellow flowers.

Kingcup or Marsh Marigold *Caltha palustris* (**3**, *shown smaller scale*) is a close relative of the buttercups. Its large yellow flowers, framed against a mass of dark green kidney-shaped leaves, are a common and striking sight in water meadows and marshy places in the spring.

MARSH AND BOG PLANTS

Bogbean *Menyanthes trifoliata* (**5**) thrusts its distinctive three-lobed leaves and erect flower stalk up into the air from a submerged creeping stem. The attractive pink and white flowers are about 15mm across and hairy within. A plant of bogs, marshes and shallow muddy pond margins.

Bog Asphodel *Narthecium ossifragum* (**4**) is a miniature lily with erect spikes of starry golden flowers which, in quantity, make a glorious display in its native uplant bogs. The leaves form a flat fan like a tiny iris.

Marsh Orchids *Dactylorhiza* spp. (**6**) bear their flowers on a fleshy spike arising from a rosette of lanceolate leaves, plain or spotted. The flowers are various shades of pink to purple, almost 2cm long, with the characteristic orchid 'lip'.

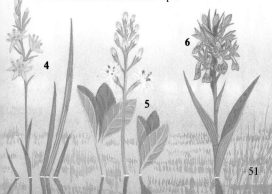

HORSETAILS

Horsetails *Equisetum* are the modern remnants of an ancient, once-dominant group of plants, some of which were important constituents of the coal measures. They consist of erect, hollow, jointed stems, usually with whorls of jointed branchlets, and small spore-bearing cones at the stem tips.

Water Horsetail *E. fluviatile* (**2**) has a thin-walled stem (**2a**) and rather few branchlets (sometimes totally absent). It often grows *in* water, forming dense beds, but also in marshy places. **Marsh Horsetail** *E. palustre* (**1**) has a thick-walled stem (**1a**) and bushier, profusely branched growth.

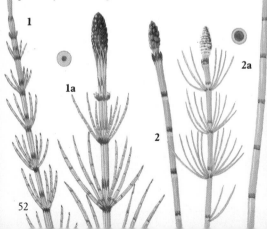

MAMMALS

Aquatic mammals, apart from 'water rats' are not a common sight in western Europe. Nowadays, sadly, the otter is a declining species, in England at least, and the introduced North American mink is more likely to be seen around inland waterways. In the past, two other American mammals became established in the wild (feral) after escaping from fur farms. Coypu (Nutria) *Myocastor coypus*, a large dog-sized rodent, and the smaller Muskrat (Musquash) *Ondantra zibethica*. Both have now been eradicated from the wild. The rare European Beaver *Castor fiber* occurs only beyond the territories covered in this book.

Water Shrew *Neomys fodiens* (**3**), our largest shrew, is widespread and fairly common. This sharp-nosed bundle of quivering energy is up to 10cm long, its tail as long again, with dense grey-brown fur above and a pale belly. It usually prefers running water but can

3

53

also be found in clean ponds and ditches, where it swims and scrabbles about underwater, searching out worms and insect larvae.

Water Vole or **'True' Water Rat** *Arvicola amphibia* (**2**) is frequently, though needlessly, confused with the Brown Rat. The vole has a blunter, broader snout, inconspicuous furry ears and a relatively short, hairy tail of only half its body length. Its body, about

1

20cm long, is a little smaller than that of the rat. The extensive burrows of the water vole often undermine steep banks, but otherwise the creature does little damage. It will soon learn to ignore a quiet, still observer, so it is fairly easy to watch it going about its business, swimming at the surface or underwater, or sitting up like a squirrel to nibble some titbit held in its forepaws.

Brown Rat *Rattus norvegicus* (**1**) is an altogether less charming beast, sharp-faced with prominent naked ears and a long scaly tail, it is an unwelcome companion of man wherever he lives throughout the world. Being a good swimmer it is almost as common around ponds as the water vole.

55

Otter *Lutra lutra* (**1**) is unmistakable, up to 1.2m long, of which a third is the stout tail, sleek mid-brown with a large white throat-and-chest patch. It has a flattish head with a broad muzzle and webbed toes.

1

2

American Mink *Mustela vison* (**2**) is now more common than the otter, smaller (scarcely half its length) and usually darker brown with only a small spot of white on the chin – though pale forms may breed true.

BIRDS

Almost any bird may turn up near or over water, so this section has been limited to those which are a characteristic part of the pond scene. Many of these birds feed in or under water, others on insects which breed in water, or on the seeds of aquatic plants. Occasional visitors, such as various waders, are not regarded as typical pond birds.

GREBE FAMILY

Grebes are typical pond birds, diving and swimming well under water to catch fishes and larger invertebrates.

1

Great Crested Grebe *Podiceps cristatus* (**2**) is a conspicuous duck-sized bird with dark crests and throat tufts in summer (less obvious in winter). During the spring its noisy territorial squabbles and courting displays can hardly be missed.

Little Grebe or **Dabchick** *Tachybaptus ruficollis* (**1**), although probably more common than the Great Crested, is small, fairly shy and easily overlooked. It is a plump, thrush-sized bird, generally dark grey-brown, the male distinguished by his chestnut chin (pale in female). When startled it will dive and swim off rapidly underwater, looking remarkably like a large frog.

RAIL FAMILY

Coot *Fulica atra* (**3**), about the size of a small duck, is our largest rail, unmistakeable in its overall blackish plumage and contrasting white forehead. It is often seen in flocks during the winter but becomes aggressively territorial in the breeding season.

Moorhen or **Waterhen** *Gallinula chloropus* (**2**) is possibly the most characteristic pond bird. Sleek blackish brown, with a red forehead, yellow bill and a white flash on tail and wings, it is usually seen stepping warily around the water's edge or on lily pads, which can just bear its weight spread over the wide extent of its enormously long toes.

Water Rail *Rallus aquaticus* (**1**) is less common and very shy, usually skulking in dense vegetation and rarely showing itself in the open. A little smaller than a moorhen but longer billed, it is a handsome bird, mottled brown above and greyish below with finely cross-banded flanks.

1

HERON AND KINGFISHER FAMILIES

Heron *Ardea cinerea* (**1**) is a timid creature, in spite of its size, and the slow, powerful beat of its retreating wings is the only sight most of us are allowed. However, a cautious early visitor may get a glimpse of this tall, stately bird posing motionless in the shallows, waiting for some unfortunate fish, frog, watervole or large insect to wander within range of its long neck and sword-like bill.

Kingfisher *Alcedo atthis* (**2**) prefers running waters, where it nests in a hole in a steep bank, but nonetheless this little bird is a frequent pond visitor and its vivid blue-green upper parts and low rapid flight make it unmistakable. With luck it may perch within view, ready to plunge headlong in pursuit of a small fish.

DUCK FAMILY (Anatidae)

Mute Swan *Cygnus olor* (**1**) is our only resident swan and scarcely requires description, save to note its red, black-knobbed bill – other swans are winter visitors with yellow unknobbed bills. Europe's largest bird is arrogantly aware of its status: breeding pairs – they mate for life – vigorously defend their nest pile of broken reeds and water plants, bullying smaller birds and even hissing and flapping at humans.

Canada Goose *Branta canadensis* (**2**), nearly as large as a swan, now probably exceeds it in numbers. It has spread rapidly as a wild bird since being introduced for domestic and decorative purposes. Distinguished from our native 'black' geese by its greater size and black neck, it is a noisy gregarious bird, grazing in waterside pastures and nesting around larger ponds and lakes.

Ducks

The commoner ducks belong to two genera: *Anas*, 'Dabblers', forage in shallow water, often up-ending themselves searching for food, and *Aythya*, which dive beneath the surface (*see page 18*). When taking off from water dabblers spring straight into the air but divers need to run along the surface to gain flying speed. Males are called drakes but females are just ducks, most of them very much alike, except to experts or drakes, and their identity must be judged by the company they keep. The same is true of ducklings, which are usually blotchy brown, unlike yellow domestic ducklings.

Mallard *Anas platyrhynchos* (**3**) the most common and best known wild duck, is an ancestor of the farmyard or 'park pond' ducks with which it may interbreed to

produce colourful variants. The drake has a glossy green-purple head and chestnut throat divided by a white clerical collar. The duck is mottled and streaked brown, broken only by a blue flash on each wing.

Teal *A. crecca* (**2**) is a pigeon-sized duck, fairly common but secretive, often nesting away from water. The brown head has a large green eye patch.

Wigeon *A. penelope* (**4**) is a little smaller than (1) and rather pale with a buff forehead on a brown head. It is mainly a winter visitor, but some breed.

Gadwall *A. strepera* (**1**) is a rather drab, uncommon, exclusively freshwater duck. Slightly smaller than (1), drakes have a black and white wing patch.

Shoveler *Anas clypeata.* (**1**), pigeon-sized, uses its distinctive broad blackish bill to scoop and sieve small invertebrates and plant matter from shallow water. It is locally distributed, preferring to feed in and nest near shallow muddy waters.

Pintail *Anas acuta* (**2**) is an elegant occasional winter visitor to larger inland waters, usually in mixed flocks with other species.

Tufted Duck *Aythya fuligula* (**3**) is a chic black and white duck common on larger bodies of water. It is gregarious and when disturbed prefers to swim further offshore rather than fly.

Pochard *Aythya ferina* (**4**) is distinguished by its greyish body, dark chest and chestnut head. Most are winter visitors but some stay to breed.

Goldeneye *Bucephala clangula* (**5**) is a common winter visitor, rarely breeding in Britain. Its large glossy green head, chestnut in ducks, has a characteristic profile. Unlike the *Aythyas* this is a diver with a springing take-off!

Goosander *Mergus merganser* (**6**) is larger than a Mallard and its slender, saw-toothed bill indicates that it is a fish-eater. It is frequently seen inland in the winter, staying to breed in the north.

SONGBIRDS

Sedge Warbler *Acrocephalus schoenobaenus* (**2**) is a shy inhabitant of reedbeds and scrubby areas near water. the pale eyestripe and dark streaks on the brown back separate it from the plainer **Reed Warbler** *A. scirpaceus* (**1**). Both species breed amongst tall reeds, drawing the stems together to support a cup-shaped nest.

Reed Bunting *Emberiza schoeniclus* (**4**), another denizen of the reed forests, is black-headed, chunkier

3   **4**

and less secretive than the warblers. The duller females can be recognised by their white outer tail feathers.

Wren *Troglodytes troglodytes* (**3**) is a friendly little bird and a frequent companion of the pondside observer, although also common in other habitats. Its small stumpy body is recognised as readily as its disproportionally loud voice and constant activity, usually near ground level, where it is often taken to be a mouse.

SWALLOWS and SWIFTS

Small birds swooping low over water, where they snap up insects on the wing, are a common feature of any area of open water in summer. The following four birds are all summer migrants and their appearance is a pleasant reminder that warm days are not far away. Before the phenomenon of migration was discovered it was a common belief that swallows, and probably martins too, spent the winter buried in mud beneath the water.

Sand martins nest communally in holes in sand cliffs, often near water, whereas swallows and house martins, naturally cliff nesters, have taken to constructing their inverted mud huts in or on houses and other buildings.

Swallow *Hirundo rustica* (**1**), best known of this group, is identified by its long, deeply forked tail and

the uniformly dark bluish back and breast band, contrasting with the pale underparts. The chestnut chin and forehead merge with the other dark colours when seen in flight.

House Martin *Delichon urbica* (**4**), also dark bluish above, has a much less deeply forked tail, totally pallid underparts and a white rump.

Sand Martin *Riparia riparia* (**3**) is distinctly paler than its House Martin relative, brownish above with a dark breast band, otherwise white below.

Swift *Apus apus* (**2**) is larger than the swallows and martins with long sickle-like wings. It is totally dusky grey-brown, apart from a slightly paler chin, and less often seen over water, although it may be present at heights where it is scarcely visible.

REPTILES

Reptiles are terrestrial animals, some of which have adapted to life in water. In western Europe there is only one, the Grass Snake, which is at all aquatic, and this only occasionally. It is perhaps with mixed feelings that we view the lack of such spectacular freshwater reptiles as crocodiles, anacondas and giant water lizards.

Grass Snake *Natrix natrix* (**1**) can grow to 150cm or more but is usually only about 1m. Its smooth scaly body is olive green or brown, often with regular dark spots or vague stripes. Many individuals show a black and yellow patch behind the 'ears' but this is not

2

constant. Grass snakes are often seen around water, basking on sunny banks or swimming with sinuous grace at the surface, as their main food is amphibians or, less often, fishes. They are equally common in fields and woods.

European Pond Terrapin *Emys orbicularis* (**2**) is the only western European tortoise, distributed mainly in the south and only just reaching northern France. Its carapace ('shell') is more smoothly rounded than the familiar land tortoises and up to 30cm long. Terrapins are almost entirely aquatic and very shy, rarely showing more than the head above the surface and diving if alarmed. The occasional specimen that turns up in our area is likely to be a deliberate introduction or an escaped pet.

AMPHIBIANS

Amphibians are so called because they are linked with water by having to breed there, but few remain aquatic outside the breeding season. They usually live in woods or damp meadows, feeding on worms and insects. Amphibians are frequently confused with reptiles (snakes, lizards, turtles) which do not breed in water and have dry scaly skins; amphibians may be smooth-skinned or warty, but are never scaly. Amphibians with tails are called newts (with many local names), whilst tailless ones are frogs or toads. Only six species are native to the British Isles but on the European mainland many more species occur, especially of frogs.

NEWTS and SALAMANDERS
The aquatic stages, including larvae (tadpoles) are shown on pages 138-41).

Great Crested or **Warty Newt** *Triturus cristatus* (**2**) is up to 15cm long, with numerous tiny warts on its skin. It varies from dark grey to blackish, with darker spots. Although officially a threatened species, through habitat destruction, this newt is still fairly frequent in small ponds in many areas. In Britain it

is **strictly protected** by law in all its stages: it must not be disturbed or collected.

Marbled Newt *T. marmoratus* (**1**) is closely related and very similar to the Crested, but basically light green with black marbling. It occurs southward from northern France.

Common or **Smooth Newt** *T. vulgaris* (**1**) is easily
the commonest lowland newt throughout our area. It
is smaller than the preceding two species, up to 11cm,
and grey-brown with many blackish spots, shading to
dull orange underneath.

Palmate Newt *T. helveticus* (**2**) is an upland version
of the Smooth Newt, preferring hilly habitats and
acidic pools, but both species overlap in many
regions, especially in acidic lowland bogs and
marshes and they are difficult to distinguish (except
breeding males, pages 140-1). Palmates are generally
a little smaller (9cm) and darker, and usually lack
spots on the throat.

Fire Salamander *Salamandra salamandra* (**3**) is a striking black and yellow terrestrial newt which can reach 16-20cm in length and lurks in moist woods and hillsides throughout mainland Europe. It occasionally lays eggs in water but more usually retains them inside the body until hatching, when the young are born alive in ponds and streams.

Alpine Newt *T. alpestris* (**4**) is about 12cm long, dark greyish becoming orange-yellow below, with numerous spots mainly on the flanks. Distributed throughout much of mainland Europe and, unlike other newts, spends much of its time in water.

4 ♂

FROGS and TOADS

These familiar animals have probably been more responsible for introducing people to the study of pond life than any others. Who has not, at some time in their childhood, taken home a few tadpoles in a jam jar – and, all too often, watched them die ?

'True' frogs, genus *Rana*, are smooth-skinned with a pair of prominent ridged skin folds along the back. Two groups of species can be defined: 'Brown frogs', including the Common Frog and its allies, which have dark ear patches and are mostly terrestrial outside the breeding season, and 'Green frogs', generally larger and lacking ear patches, and habitually aquatic.

Breeding frogs, spawn and tadpoles are shown on pages 142-3.

BROWN FROGS

Moor Frog *Rana arvalis* (**1**), found north- and eastward from northern France, is distinctly shorter-legged than the other brown frogs, sparsely spotted beneath, and may have dark stripes on its back.

Common Frog *Rana temporaria* (**3**), about 6-9cm long and blunt-nosed compared to Agile and Moor Frogs (preceding and below), occurs in a wide range of colours (not green!) from brown to yellow, usually with dark blotches and spots above and below. It breeds in early spring, typically March in Britain but varying according to the weather. This species occurs throughout our area, overlapping in northern France with the following close relatives.

Agile Frog *R. dalmatina* (**2**), found south- and eastward from northern France, is long-legged, frequently yellow around the genital region, rarely spotted underneath.

GREEN FROGS

Green frogs are characteristic of wetlands throughout Europe, except in the U.K. (where introduced populations seem to be thriving). They are active and noisy night and day, hopping into water when disturbed, but in spite of their size and constant calling individuals can be difficult to locate.

Marsh Frog *R. ridibunda* (**1**) is the largest European native, up to 15cm, variable in colour but typically with some green visible, usually marbled or overshaded with brown. The **Pool Frog** *R. lessonae* (**2**) is smaller, about 9cm, and differs by having yellow or orange patches behind its legs. Interbreeding between these two has produced the confusing range of intermediate hybrids called **Edible Frogs** *R. esculenta*. Unusually, these hybrids can interbreed with either parent species to make more Edible Frogs. It is not only those called Edible Frogs that 'gourmets' like, any frog large enough to eat qualifies as 'Grenouille'.

Common Toad *Bufo bufo* (**3**) may become as long as 15cm but is usually about 7-10cm. It is easily recognised by its rough warty brown skin, horizontal eye pupil and rather weak hind legs – it cannot jump, only hop feebly or walk.

Natterjack Toad *B. calamita* (**4**), a little smaller and much less common than *B. bufo*, is identified by the yellow centre stripe down its back. Habitat destruction has reduced its numbers to a few isolated populations, mainly in coastland and dune areas in the British Isles (where it now enjoys the same protected status as the Crested Newt) but it fares a little better on the continent.

3

4

In mainland Europe:

Here other species enter the picture. The following five species are widely distributed through the continental part of our area, and basically terrestrial outside the brief mating season.

Yellow-bellied Toad *Bombina variegata* (**2**) has brownish, rough warty skin like *B. bufo*, but a rounded eye pupil. Its bright yellow-orange underside, variegated with brown or grey, instantly identifies this little (5cm) toad.

Midwife Toad *Alytes obstetricans* (**1**), also about 5cm, is brown or grey with darker mottling, and a vertical eye pupil. Its name derives from the males' curious habit of carrying the eggs in a mass attached to its rump, not depositing them in water until near to hatching.

Tree Frog *Hyla arborea* (**3**) is an agile little creature about 4cm long and typically bright green, although capable of changing to brown or yellow to match different surroundings. It lives in bushes or reedbeds, often near the water where it breeds. A southern species with its northern limits in France, there is a small introduced population just surviving in southern England.

Parsley Frog *Pelodytes punctatus* (**4**), about 5cm, resembles the Midwife Toad but is more slender, longer-legged and does not carry its eggs.

Spadefoot Toad *Pelobates fuscus* (**5**) is a fat, smooth-skinned, 10cm toad, very variable in colour, with vertical eye pupil and a hard flat callus (the 'spade') on each hind foot.

INSECTS

Insects are animals with hardened skins forming an external skeleton, like a suit of armour. Adults possess three pairs of legs and usually have two pairs of wings (sometimes only one, sometimes absent). The body is divided into three main regions: head, which bears a pair of antennae; thorax, to which wings and legs are attached; and the often softer abdomen, which usually lacks appendages but may have 'tails' of various types.

Juvenile insects differ from their mature forms and are often unrecognisable as being the same animal. In order to understand them it is helpful to know something of their varied and complex life cycles, of which there are two main kinds.

The first type includes Mayflies, Dragonflies and Bugs. From the egg hatches a *nymph* (**1a**), which is more or less similar in form to the adult, but wingless. As they grow, nymphs must cast off (moult) their skins, like children growing out of their clothes. Older nymphs increasingly resemble their parents and develop wing buds. During the final moult they 'hatch' into winged adults (**1**).

Insects of the second group, Flies (**2**), Beetles (**3**), Moths and others, have young called *larvae*, the familiar maggots and caterpillars, or the less well known but more active beetle larvae (**3a**) and mosquito larvae (**2a**). Larvae rarely resemble their parents in shape. They too moult as they grow and when full grown become *pupae* – inactive cocoons (*chrysalids*) or, less commonly, active free-swimming creatures (**4**). The pupa is a transitional stage during which the larval body changes (*metamorphoses*) into that of an adult. Eventually the pupal skin or cocoon is shed and a new adult emerges. Newly hatched adults are soft and pallid at first, allowing them to expand their wings before they harden off in the air.

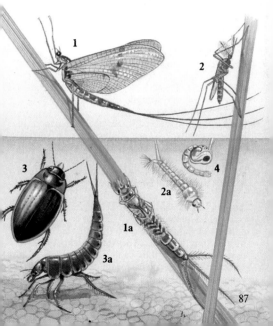

Mayflies (Ephemeroptera)

These are the only insects to moult from a first winged stage (*sub-imago*) to a second, the mature adult or *imago*. They are delicate with large gauzy forewings, small hindwings (sometimes absent) and two or three slender tails. The nymphs (pages 173-4) are always aquatic and adults, being weak fliers, rarely travel far from water unless wind blown.

Mature nymphs swim to the surface to moult ('hatch') into the dull sub-imago ('dun' to anglers) which very soon sheds its skin to reveal the shimmering, translucent imago (the anglers' 'spinner'). After mating which follows an enchanting courtship flight, the females drop their eggs into the water and die. This brief (ephemeral) adult life gives rise to the group's scientific name.

Pond Olives *Chloeon* (**3**) are the commonest of lowland mayflies. There are two similar species, about 7-10mm long and readily identified by their single pair of wings and only two tails. Sub-imagos are dull olive but the imago varies from yellowish to brilliant orange with amber wings.

Anglers' Curse *Caenis* (**4**, many species) is so called because its diminutive size, 5mm or less, makes it difficult for the angler to catch trout that are obsessed with feeding on them. They have a single pair of broad wings and three tails. Hatches are often spectacular evening affairs with tens of thousands appearing suddenly as if by magic.

Claret Dun *Leptophlebia* (**2**) is often the only mayfly present in upland areas as it prefers peaty acidic water. It has a dark reddish body, 9-12mm long, two pairs of wings and three tails.

Greendrake *Ephemera* (**1**) is our largest mayfly, up to 25mm long, easily distinguished by its pale cream colour. Usually a stream dweller, it sometimes breeds in gravel-bottomed ponds.

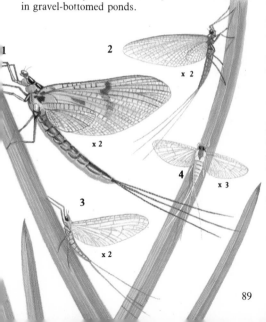

1

2

x 2

x 2

4

x 3

3

x 2

DRAGONFLIES and DAMSELFLIES (Odonata)

Dragonflies are large and conspicuous insects. With their smaller cousins, the Damselflies, they form a single group characterised by elongated bodies, large eyes, strong jaws and two pairs of roughly equal wings which cannot be folded. Despite superstitions such as the name 'horse stingers' they are harmless to people and livestock. They hatch from ferocious nymphs that are always aquatic. Both are common around water but dragonflies, being much stronger fliers, may wander far in search of prey which consists of smaller insects caught on the wing in the basket formed by the legs, the captor perching to eat. Mating takes place either perched or in flight, couples often assuming an athletic position known as a copulation wheel (**1, Common Darters**, see page 95). Females lay their eggs on or inside plants, either above or in water, sometimes actually crawling beneath the surface to accomplish this. The adult life-span may

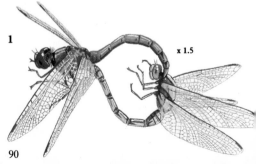

1

x 1.5

last up to eight weeks, but two or three is more usual. Coloration varies with age and full brilliance may take a week or two to develop. Old females may assume male coloration.

DRAGONFLIES

All are robust insects, powerful and swift in flight, resting with their wings held horizontally. Hawker dragonflies are the largest, 6-8cm long, with cylindrical abdomens.

Emperor Dragonfly *Anax imperator* (**2**), a southern species, is distinguished by its green thorax and dark

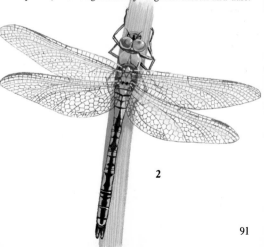

2

mid-line on the abdomen, which is blue in males, blue-green in females.

Common Hawker *Aeshna juncea* (**1**) has slanted yellow stripes on the sides of its thorax, a dusky abdomen with blue spots in males, yellow or green spots in females. *A. mixta* resembles *juncea* but has broad yellow patches on the sides of the thorax.

Southern Hawker *A. cynea* (**2**) has vivid yellow-green markings on its dusky body, the green stripes on the thorax being characteristic.

Brown Hawker *A. grandis* (**3**) is unmistakeable: very large, 8-10cm or more, with brown body and amber-tinted wings (other hawkers have colourless wings).

1

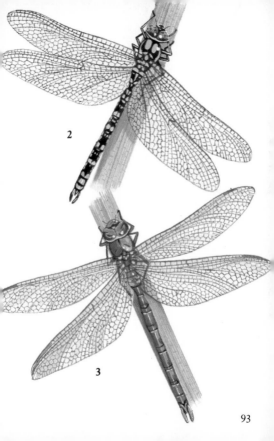

2

3

Chaser dragonflies have more or less flattened abdomens and are smaller than hawkers, typically 4-5cm. They spend less time on the wing, preferring to wait in ambush, making short dashes to intercept passing prey.

Broad-bodied Chaser *Libellula depressa* (**4**) has the widest abdomen – blue in males, buff in females – and a dark blotch at each wing base.

Four-spotted Chaser *L. quadrimaculata* (**1**) has a brown body, lacks a basal blotch on the forewings and has a characteristic spot midway along each wing.

Black-tailed Skimmer *Orthetrum cancellatum* (**2**) has a narrower abdomen than *Libellula*, yellow with black

markings in the female, blue with a dusky tip in males.

Darter dragonflies are small, rarely exceeding 4cm, with cylindrical or club-shaped bodies.

Black Darter *Sympetrum danae* (**3**) males are black, females brown or buff, both with black legs. It is found mostly in upland bogs and marshy areas.

Common Darter *S. striolatum* (*illustrated page 90 (1)*) is a little larger, up to 4cm, with a dull red abdomen in males, yellowish in females.

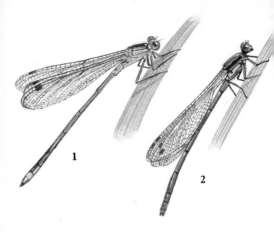

DAMSELFLIES
These are slenderer, more delicate creatures than dragonflies, usually more abundant but less obvious. Although good fliers, they are comparatively slow and spend much time at rest, when the wings are closed together above the back (half-open in the Emerald). All the common pond species have clear wings – the metallic blue demoiselles, with dark wing patches breed only in streams.

Emerald Damsel *Lestes sponsa* (**1**) has a metallic green body, up to 4cm long. A local but widespread species.

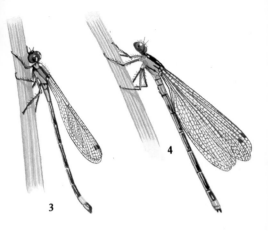

all illustrations x 1.5

Large Red Damsel *Pyrrhosoma nymphula* (**2**) is about 3.5cm long. Its abdomen is red with black markings and other parts black with red marks; legs are black.

Blue-tailed Damsel *Ischnura elegans* (**3**), 3-3.5cm, is blackish with a blue band near the tail and stripes of varied colour on the thorax.

Red-eyed Damsel *Erythromma najas* (**4**) is very similar but it is larger at 3.5-4cm, its thorax is plain black and the eyes red.

Azure Damsel *Coenagrion puella* (**2**), 3-3.5cm, has bright blue males with blackish markings – note the U-shaped mark on the back. Females vary from blackish to yellowish-olive.

Common Blue *Enallagma cyathigera* (**1**) resembles the Azure Damsel but lacks the U-shaped mark. Females are yellowish or greenish.

MOTHS

Moths are frequently seen around water but it is not widely known that some, China-mark Moths and others, have aquatic caterpillars.

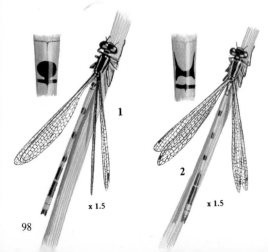

1

2

x 1.5

x 1.5

Bulrush Wainscot Moth *Nonagria typhae* (**3**) is a common waterside insect in late summer and autumn, although not strictly aquatic. The female inserts her eggs into a slit cut in a Reedmace *Typha* stem. These hatch the following spring, the large flesh-coloured caterpillars feeding inside the stem and eventually pupating in the cavities they have eaten (**3a**).

China-mark Moths *Nymphula* (**4**) are small, up to 3cm wingspan, with white or cream wings crisply marked in dark brown. *Their larvae are shown on page 185.*

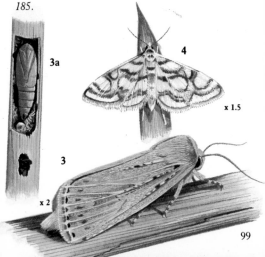

3a

4

x 1.5

3

x 2

SEDGE or CADDIS FLIES (Trichoptera)

These are the winged adult stages of our well-known aquatic caddis grubs (*page 182-4*). Superficially they resemble moths but their wings are hairy, not scaly, and typically held like a pitched roof over the back. A pair of long antennae points forward. Unlike moths they are nimble footed and often prefer running to flight. Sedges are common insects around water during the warmer months, often appearing in great numbers, especially at dusk. Newly hatched adults can make quite a commotion as they run and flutter along the surface, making for the cover of bankside vegetation where most hide during the day. Others, such as silverhorns, fly more readily and are more prominent in daytime.

Differences between species are often slight so common names often apply to several similar species.

Longhorn *Oecetis* (**2**) is closely related to silverhorns, with brown wings and very long antennae (3 x body).

Mottled Sedge *Glypholaelius pellucidus* (**1**), at about 20mm a little smaller than the Great Red, is yellowish blotched brown.

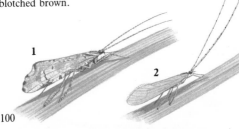

100

Brown Sedge covers a multitude of medium sized species (15-25mm long) in many genera: *Anabolia*, **Halesus** (**4**), *Molanna*, *Limnephilus* (the largest genus) and others. Shades of brown vary and wing markings may be present or absent.

Silverhorns form another composite group including *Athripsodes*, **Mystacides** (**3**), *Triaenodes*, and *Leptocerus*. They are all smallish, 8-10mm, slender sedges with noticeably long antennae. Wings range from black to pale brown.

Great Red Sedge *Phryganea grandis* (**5**) is our largest species, about 30mm long, its wings reddish with brown markings.

all illustrations x 1.5

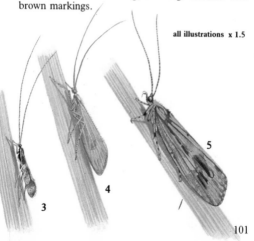

3

4

5

SPONGEFLIES (Neuroptera)

Spongeflies *Sisyra* (**1**) resemble tiny lacewings about 4mm long. They are not often seen, due to their small size and secretive habits, but stay close to water. The larvae (*page 182*) are aquatic, living on sponges, leaving the water to pupate in crevices nearby.

ALDERFLY (Megaloptera)

Alderfly *Sialis lutraria* (**2**) is a distinctive dark bodied insect about 12-15mm with strongly veined wings. It spends most of its time hiding in bankside vegetation. The larva (*page 182*) are aquatic, but leave the water in spring to pupate in damp soil.

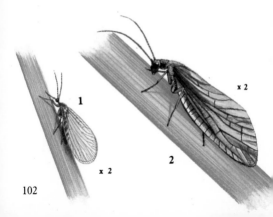

x 2

1

2

x 2

BEETLES (Coleoptera)

Most 'true' water beetles spend much of their time in water, although leaving it to fly during warm weather, but a few species are exclusively terrestrial as adults and aquatic as larvae. Whirligig Beetles, so conspicuous *on* the water, are described on pages 111 and 189.

x 3

3

Leaf Beetle *Donacia vulgaris* (**3**), one of several leaf beetles, is frequently seen on various marginal plants. It has an angular body about 10mm long, metallic and iridescent green shot with other hues. Its fat maggot-like larvae can be found attached to the roots of water plants where it also pupates (*see page 199*).

TRUE FLIES (Diptera)

True flies, which include the familiar houseflies and bluebottles, have only one pair of wings (hence Diptera = two-winged). Many kinds have aquatic larvae but only the various midges and mosquitoes are commonly associated with water as adults. Their presence in large numbers can be intensely irritating to humans, whether they bite or not.

PLUMED GNATS (Chironomidae)

These form a huge family to which the commonest midges belong. All are very similar in appearance: slender bodies, long legs, narrow wings and large feathery antennae (**1a, b**). Sizes range from almost microscopic to about 1cm and many different colours occur. Their larvae are the bloodworms so frequent in water butts and other such places (*page 186*). Chironomids often appear in vast swarms, creating a loud buzzing that rarely fails to cause alarm, but fortunately they do not bite.

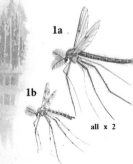

1a

1b

all x 2

MOSQUITOES or GNATS (Culicidae)

Mosquitoes, with their dull leaden bodies and fearsome stilleto-like mouthparts, are the best known waterborne flies. The female's unpleasant habit (to us!) of feeding on human blood has caused the spread of malaria and other major diseases. Only the females are blood suckers, needing this nutrient to make eggs; males are harmless nectar feeders. Sexes can be distinguished, when the proboscis is not actually plunged into you, by the female's sparsely haired antennae in comparison with the male's bushier, sometimes feathery ones. The larvae and interesting, free-swimming pupae (*page 187*) are always aquatic.

Malarial Mosquito *Anopheles* (**2**) differs from the others by its 'tail-up' resting stance with proboscis held straight ahead. Some species have spotted wings.

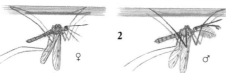

2 ♀ ♂

Theobaldia (**3**) is our largest mosquito, with spotted wings and bold pale rings around the leg joints. It is frequently found in houses where it is only too willing to sample human blood donors.

♀ 3 ♂

105

Culex (1) and *Aedes* (2) are difficult to tell apart, except that females of the latter have a more tapered, pointed abdomen than the former. *Aedes* is a vicious biter, breeding mostly in small water bodies such as tree holes, temporary pools and ditches. *Culex* is relatively harmless and rarely bites people, although common around houses where it often breeds in water butts and gutters.

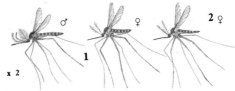

x 2

BITING MIDGES (Ceratopogonidae)

Midges (3) are more often a nuisance around ponds than mosquitoes. they are tiny hump-backed flies only 2-3mm long, with a bite out of all proportion to their size! Many have aquatic larvae (*page 188*).

x 4

Several other types of True Flies include species with aquatic larvae, although the adults are not particularly associated with water. Some of the **Crane Flies** (**4**) or Daddy-long-legs, have larvae that live in ponds, as does a **Hover Fly** *Eristalis* (**5**) and some of the **Horse Flies** (**6**), perhaps the most loathed of all biting flies (*larva page 188*).

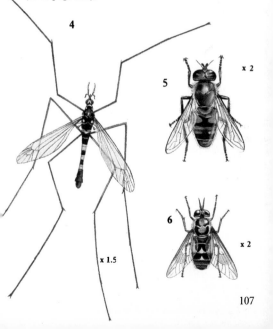

4

5

x 2

6

x 2

x 1.5

SNAILS

The damp margins of ponds, just above the water line, form an ideal habitat for snails and many true land snails turn up here. The two below, however, are specialists that live nowhere else. Some aquatic snails (including *Lymnaea truncatula*, *L. palustris* and *Aplexa hypnorum*, pages 212-14) leave the water readily or inhabit places that dry up frequently. They are often found above the water line, especially on plant stems or patches of mud left by the receding water.

Amber Snail *Succinea putris* (**1**) has a glossy delicate translucent shell, up to 20mm tall, into which its succulent body cannot be wholly withdrawn. This snail is common in marshes and reedbeds, sometimes becoming temporarily stranded on emergent plant stems during times of flood – it will drown if submerged for long.

Zonitoides nitidus (**2**) is a small snail with a flattish shell, up to 8mm across, found close to water in low vegetation, marshlands and similar places. Although sometimes called the Shiny snail, it is no glossier than many others.

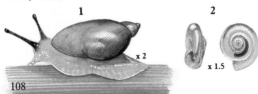

1

x 2

2

x 1.5

The water surface

The water surface is a barrier that has to be penetrated by the many underwater animals that need to breathe atmospheric air and by those insects with aquatic young that hatch into adults at the surface. It is also a strange, two-dimensional world inhabited by a scattering of specialised animals and plants.

INSECTS

Springtails (Collembola) are the tiniest animal inhabitants of this zone. Also common in soils and leaf litter, they are primitive wingless insects that can jump relatively huge distances by means of a spring-loaded lever under their tails. *Podura aquatica* (**3**), about 1mm long and dark blue-grey, is probably the most common. The larger, yellowish *Isotomurus palustris* (**4**) may reach 2.5mm.

These and other smaller species can be very common scavenging amongst floating debris at pond margins but require close inspection to find them. They are active all year round, even in icy conditions.

x 10

3

4

3

BUGS

Water Bugs divide neatly into those that live submerged (but may leave the water to fly) and the surface dwelling specialists, which may be winged or wingless but in any case rarely fly.

Water Measurer *Hydrometra* (**3**) is common but easy to miss. Slender and up to 12mm long, it strides across the surface, sometimes running, rarely straying far from the cover of marginal plantlife, and spears small aquatic creatures through the surface with its long pointed nose (rostrum).

Water Crickets *Velia* (**1**) sometimes occur in pools, although more typical of running waters. Smaller, up to 8mm, and broader bodied than water skaters (*below*), some have two red stripes along the body. Like water skaters they are fast moving hunters of insects that become bogged down in the surface film.

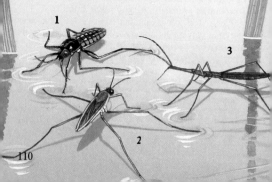

Water Skaters *Gerris* (**2**) are common in all still waters but active only in warmer weather, dimpling the surface in conspicuous fashion as they sprint across it in short spurts. Up to 17mm long and very long-legged, they differ from other surface bugs by the large gap between the first and second pair of legs.

BEETLES

In warm weather Whirligig beetles can be the most conspicuous surface dwellers, hurtling around ahead of a prominent wake (**4**). However, they also spend much time submerged so are described in detail, along with their aquatic larvae, on page 189.

SPIDERS

Raft Spider *Dolomedes fimbriatus* (**5**) is a handsome beast. One of Britain's largest and rarest spiders, it lurks on the surface of a few remote fens and marshes. It may enter water to hide or to catch insects and small fishes; it has even been known to snatch prey through the surface whilst reposing on a floating leaf.

PLANTS

DUCKWEEDS

These are strange little plants with no obvious stem or leaves, consisting merely of a frond of green, sometimes with a root or two hanging down but never rooted. Most float on the surface, multiplying rapidly by budding, often forming a dense carpet that hides the water beneath.

Great Duckweed *Spirodela polyrhiza* (**1**) forms oval plates up to 8mm long, red underneath and with several roots.

Common Duckweed *Lemna minor* (**2**) is similar but smaller, up to 4mm, green beneath and with only a single root.

Fat Duckweed *L. gibba* (**3**) is just that! – a green oval plate, up to 5mm long, atop a frothy whitish mass (like foam polystyrene), with a single root.

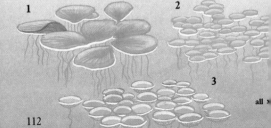

1   2

3

all ›

Ivy-leaved Duckweed *L. trisculca* (**5**) is very different. The fronds are racquet-shaped and translucent, up to 10mm long, each with a single root, budding and overlapping at right angles. This species rarely floats, forming free masses or lodging in other vegetation.

Rootless Duckweed *Wolffia arrhiza* (**4**) is the tiniest and least common of the lot, forming rootless oval specks less than 1mm long.

Water Fern *Azolla filiculoides* (**6**) is an introduced species with similar habits to duckweeds. It consists of a floating, branched frond with tiny scale-like 'leaves', green strongly tinted red-bronze.

Crystalwort *Riccia fluitans* (**7**) is a liverwort, related to the mosses (*page 134*). Its distinctive branched rootless fronds float free or tangle with other plants. A southern species.

4

5

6

7

WATER-LILIES and FROGBIT

Yellow Water-lily *Nuphar lutea* (**2**) has heart-shaped floating leaves and, usually, cabbage-like submerged ones; the yellow flowers are about 5-6cm across.

White Water-lily *Nymphaea alba* (**1**) has more rounded leaves and huge flowers 15-20cm across. An uncommon species except were it is planted for decorative purposes.

Fringed Water-lily *Nymphoides peltata* (**3**) is a lily-like relative of the Bogbean. Its small leaves, 5-8cm across, are often faceted and the yellow, conspicuously hairy flowers are borne in small clusters. In Britain it occurs mainly in the south and is becoming uncommon.

Frogbit *Hydrocharis morsus-ranae* (**4**) has kidney shaped leaves 2-3cm across and white, yellow-centred flowers held aloft on separate stems. The plants float free and spread by submerged runners. Distribution as (**3**).

Underwater Life

This section includes all the animals and plants that live more or less permanently underwater. Many of the plants carry their flowers on aerial stems; some insects may leave the water, especially in warm weather, others live underwater only during their young stages.

PLANTS

WATER CROWFOOTS

Water Crowfoots are white-flowered members of the large genus *Ranunculus*, which includes our common buttercups; all are five-petalled. Their stems are usually creeping or trailing, with lobed aerial or floating leaves and finely divided submerged ones – one or both types may be present.

Ivy-leaved Crowfoot *R. hederaceus* (**2**) has a creeping stem and only aerial leaves, rounded and three- or five-lobed with small (5mm) flowers. It is common in shallow water or on bankside mud.

Pond and **Common Water Crowfoot** *R. peltatus* (**4**) and *R. aquatilis* (**3**) are similar, rather variable and easily confused: *peltatus* has larger flowers, usually 20-25mm across, and scalloped, typically three-lobed leaves; *aquatilis* flowers are usually less than 20mm and its aerial leaves are jaggedly toothed; submerged leaves of both are too variable to separate easily. Both are common in ponds and *aquatilis* also occurs in running water.

Round-leaved Crowfoot *R. omiophyllus* (**1**) occurs only in calcium-free waters, mainly in the west and south. It has only aerial leaves, three- or five-lobed and rounded 10mm-wide flowers.

117

PONDWEEDS

Pondweeds *Potamogeton* are true aquatic plants with long floppy stems, often branched, and alternate leaves of varied form. The inconspicuous greenish flowers usually form a small emergent spike.

PLANTS WITH FLOATING AND SUBMERGED LEAVES:

Broad-leaved Pondweed *P. natans* (**1**), a very common species, has slender tape-like submerged leaves and long-stalked oval floating ones.

Bog Pondweed *P. polygonifolius* (**2**), common in acid upland waters, is similar to (1) but its submerged leaves have small oval blades.

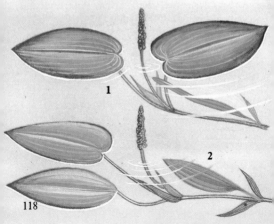

PLANTS WITH SUBMERGED LEAVES ONLY:

Perfoliate Pondweed *P. perfoliatus* (**5**) is easily recognized by its broad pale leaves embracing the stem at their bases.

Shining Pondweed *P. lucens* (**3**) has almost stalkless spear-shaped leaves of shiny translucent green.

Curled Pondweed *P. crispus* (**4**) has narrower, serrated, permanently-waved leaves of richer green.

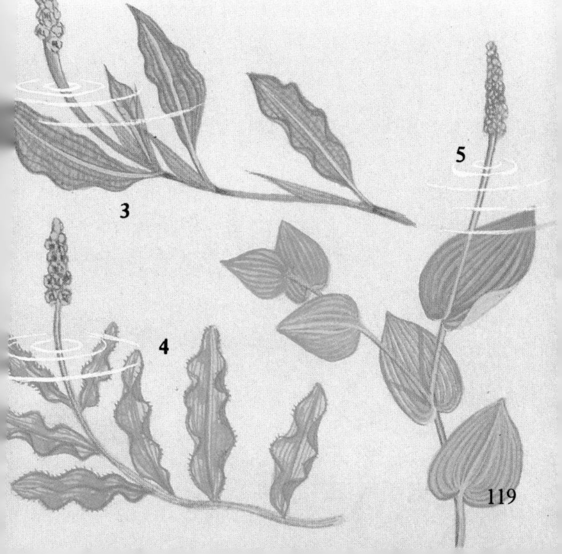

The many species with narrow leaves under 4mm wide are difficult to identify. These three are the most common:

Fennel Pondweed *P. pectinatus* (**1**) has a much-branched stem and slender leaves up to 10cm x 2mm. consisting of two parallel tubes (visible under a hand lens) with pointed tips.

Small Pondweed *P. berchtoldii* (**2**) is less profusely branched than (**1**) with flat, blunt tipped leaves up to 5cm x 2mm.

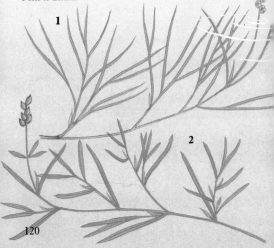

Blunt-leaved Pondweed *P. obtusifolius* (**3**) is larger than (1) with flat, blunt-tipped leaves up to 4mm wide with a distinct midrib.

Opposite-leaved Pondweed *Groenlandia densa* (**4**) resembles *Potamogeton* but its unstalked leaves arise in pairs, not alternately; they are pale green with finely serrated edges. It is mostly found in clear calcareous waters in the south.

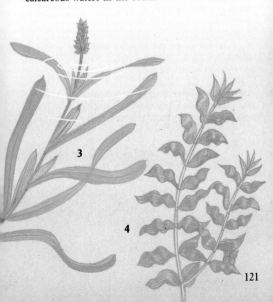

Canadian Pondweed or **Water Thyme** *Elodea canadensis* (**1**) has a long brittle stem with mid-green, blunt-tipped leaves about 10-15 x 2-4mm, arranged in whorls of three (sometimes two). The growth form is very variable, from stringy to bushy, leaves straight or curled back like (**3**). This is the commonest of several species introduced from abroad in recent times. When it first appeared it spread like a plague, often choking canals and rivers, but has now settled down as a widespread resident.

E. nuttalli (**2**) is more locally distributed. Compared to (1) its leaves are paler, softer and more slender – up to 20 x 2mm – with a longer, sharper point, and arranged in whorls of three (occasionally four).

Curly Water Thyme *Lagarosiphon major* (**3**) is darker and coarser than (1) or (2) with a thick (3-4mm) stem and pointed leaves that curl back to the stem.

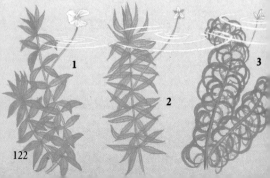

MARE'S-TAIL and WATER VIOLET

Mare's-tail *Hippuris vulgaris* (**4**) has a stout fleshy stem with whorls of 6-12 bright green strap-like leaves up to 5cm long. The firmly-rooted submerged stems often form dense beds; their tips emerge from the water when bearing the tiny green flowers in the leaf axils. (Do not confuse with horsetails, page 52, which have whorls of cylindrical branchlets.)

Water Violet *Hottonia palustris* (**5**) is really an aquatic Primrose! It has much divided leaves, up to 10cm long, and 2cm pink flowers on emergent spikes.

4

5

BLADDERWORTS

Bladderworts *Utricularia* are rootless, long-stemmed plants with finely divided leaves. Some parts bear pip-shaped bladders which are used to trap tiny swimming animals, such as water fleas: these are 'digested' to help the plant live in habitats where nutrients are scarce – they typically occur in acidic marsh or bog pools. Attractive large-lipped yellow flowers appear on aerial stems in late summer.

Common Bladderwort *U. vulgaris* (**1**) has all leaves similar, up to 5cm long, bearing 2-3mm bladders.

1

Intermediate Bladderwort *U. intermedia* (**2**) is of similar stature but rarely has bladders on the leaves, instead these are borne on leafless branches descending into the mud. It is uncommon, occuring mostly in the north.

Least Bladderwort *U. minor* (**3**) is a much smaller plant with leaves less than 15mm and tiny bladders, typically found in peaty bog pools.

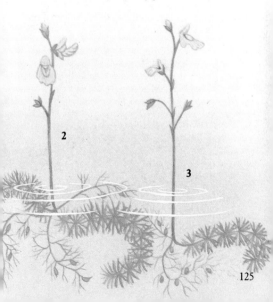

WATER MILFOILS

Water Milfoils *Myriophyllum* are submerged plants with whorls of finely divided leaves on long, trailing, rooted stems. Identification relies mainly on the form of the emergent flower spikes.

Spiked Milfoil *M. spicatum* (**1**), probably the commonest species, especially in calcareous waters, has 3-4cm long leaves in whorls of four on a 2-3mm diameter stem. Tiny reddish flowers (and later, fruits) occur in whorls of five on the spike, each with a tiny green *bract* (**a**) underneath.

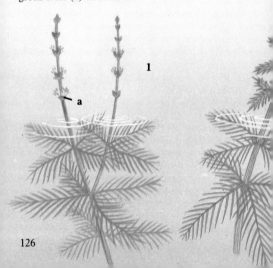

Whorled Milfoil *M. verticillatum* (**2**) is like (1) but may have five leaves per whorl. The flowers occur in whorls of four or five with large (1cm) bracts resembling miniature leaves.

Alternate-flowered Milfoil *M. alterniflorum* (**3**) is usually more delicate than (1) or (2) with leaves in fours, often slightly reddish. The flowers are arranged irregularly, typically alternate except for the lowest which may be in whorls, and with bracts graduated in size. This plant is usually found in acidic waters.

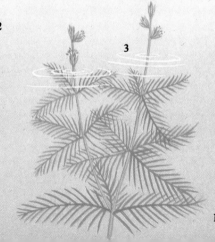

2

3

HORNWORTS and STONEWORTS

Hornworts *Ceratophyllum* are rootless submerged plants with finely divided leaves in whorls on a long brittle stem. Flowers are tiny and rarely seen.

Common Hornwort *C. demersum* (**1**) is dark green with a rather harsh texture and toothed, up-curved, twice-forked leaves.

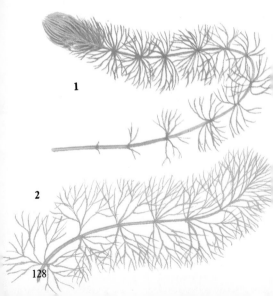

C. submersum (**2**) is rarer than (1), with softer, paler thrice-forked leaves.

Stoneworts are large algae (*see pages 136-7*) resembling 'real' plants in form and stature. They consist of long stems (made up of huge cells often more than 1cm long!) with whorls of branchlets at the joints. The fruits are tiny orange or white bodies on the branchlets. Species are hard to identify but the two main genera are fairly distinct.

Chara (**3**) is pale green and relatively stout with *unforked* branchlets; it usually grows in calcareous water and is often encrusted with limescale, giving it a crunchy texture – hence the group name.

Nitella (**4**) is more delicate than (3), usually dark green, and has long forked branchlets; it usually grows in non-calcareous waters and therefore is rarely lime-encrusted.

3

4

STARWORTS and BLINKS

Starworts *Callitriche* are very common aquatic plants which sometimes grow out of the water on to marginal muds. A slender stem bears pairs of pale green leaves of varied shape, spaced out below but forming a dense, darker rosette at the growing tip. Flowers are tiny and inconspicuous.

Common Starwort *C. stagnalis* (**1**) has club-shaped lower leaves, slightly notched at the tip and broader, often almost circular leaves in the rosette.

C. obtusangulata (**2**) has lower leaves that are more nearly parallel-sided and diamond-shaped ones forming the rosette.

1   2

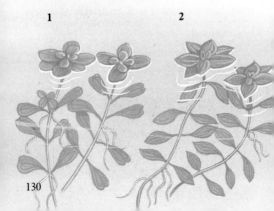

C. intermedia (or ***C. hamulata,* 4**) also has parallel-sided lower leaves but these are deeply notched at the tip, like a spanner; upper leaves similar or broader. It is usually found in acid or upland waters.

Blinks *Montia fontana* (**3**) is superficially similar to starwort but the narrow spoon-shaped, paired leaves do not form dense rosettes at the tip and the tiny white flowers are borne on long stalks. It is rarely found submerged, usually growing on waterside mud.

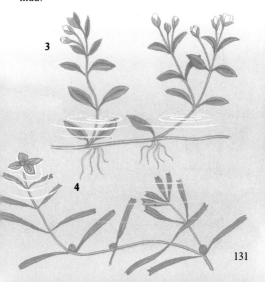

ROOTED PLANTS WITH SPIKY ROSETTES

Several different aquatic plants grow in this form, most of them inhabiting the sandy or stony bottoms of upland waters.

Shoreweed *Littorella uniflora* (**1**) has solid leaves, semi-circular in cross section, tapering only at the tips and up to 10cm long. The curious flowers are carried on a short stalk, usually when the plants are exposed by low water levels in summer. It also reproduces by runners, frequently forming a dense turf.

Awlwort *Subularis aquatica* (**3**) has solid three-angled leaves, usually less than 5cm long, tapering evenly to the tips; small white four-petalled flowers appear on erect stalks.

Water Lobelia *Lobelia dortmanna* (**2**) has 5-8cm long, fleshy but hollow, curved-back leaves and pinkish-mauve flowers on a tall emergent stem.

Quillworts *Isoetes* are aquatic ferns with spiky *spongy* leaves swollen at the base, where a tiny spore-case is hidden. **Common Quillwort** *I. lacustris* (**4**) has stiff dark green leaves up to 20cm long. Spring Quillwort *I echinospora*, with softer, paler leaves, is much less common.

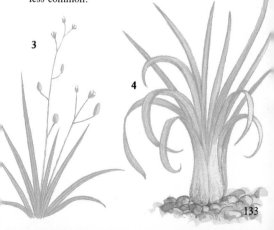

3

4

133

MOSSES (Bryophyta)
These are simple non-flowering plants, producing spores instead of seeds, and consisting of a thin stem bearing small, usually irregularly arranged leaves.

Willow Moss *Fontinalis antipyretica* (**2**) has distinctive boat-shaped (keeled) dark green leaves arranged clearly in three rows. It is one of the largest mosses.

Cinclidotus fontinaloides (**3**) is almost as large as (**2**) and like it is found in ponds or rivers. Its flattish leaves have a midrib and thickened rim.

Leptodictyon riparium (**1**) has sharply pointed leaves with an incomplete midrib. It often grows in loose masses tangled with other plants in lowland pools.

Drepanocladus aduncus (**4**) is similar to (3) but more slender and with curved or hooked leaves, and found in ponds and marshes. ***D. fluitans*** is an acid water or upland relative with yellower leaves, sometimes turning reddish.

Bog Mosses *Sphagnum* (**5**) include many similar species, all with long fleshy stems with numerous leaf-bearing side branches; the top of the stem forms a dense rosette, tinged with red in many species. *Sphagnum* typically grows in dense cushion-like clumps which are capable of retaining a large amount of water, hence they play an important part in maintaining the saturated conditions in bogs.

4

5

ALGAE

Algae are simple plants that live only in water or wet habitats. The vast majority are too small to be seen individually but many form colonies of substantial size. Almost any slimy or velvety patch of green, brown or blackish hue on a submerged or wet surface is likely to be an algal colony. At the other extreme the Stoneworts (*page 129*) are highly developed algae, almost as complex as flowering plants.

The most primitive forms are the **Blue-green Algae** which are really bacteria that function as plants. Some form dark green to black slimy patches on rocks (**1**) or other surfaces. Another kind may be responsible for *water blooms* that discolour the water or form a floating scum like spilt greenish paint (**2**).

'True' algae are real plants. Some of these form hair-like green threads by linking together end-to-end. These *filamentous algae* can become tens of centimetres long and form large tangled masses. Two common types are ***Spirogyra*** (**5**) – pale green with a slimy texture, growing unattached – and ***Cladophora*** (**3**), dark green, rough to the touch, forming skeins attached to stones or sunken branches. The largest freshwater algae is probably the wonderfully named **Green Gut-weed** *Enteromorpha intestinalis* (**6**) which makes wriggly, intestine-like tubes up to 2cm wide and a metre or more long, usually floating due to trapped gas bubbles. ***Chaetophora*** (**4**) forms round blobs or tree-like growths of green jelly, up to 10mm across, on reed stems and other surfaces.

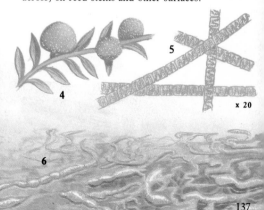

5

x 20

4

6

AMPHIBIANS

All amphibians come to water to breed and it is in water that their eggs hatch into larval stages (tadpoles) and develop into the adult forms, though adults of most kinds may spend most of the year away from the pond.

NEWTS and SALAMANDERS

Male newts develop crests and special coloration during the breeding season and these forms are shown here. The females lay single eggs, usually wrapped in the leaf of an aquatic plant (**1a**), which hatch into larvae equipped with feathery gills (**1b**). Newt larvae assume the adult shape gradually over a period of months, during which the legs appear (**1c**) and the gills are absorbed, and often remain in the pond for their first winter.

1

Great Crested or **Warty Newt** *Triturus cristatus* (**1**) is up to 15cm long. In the breeding season (April-May in U.K.) males bear a splendid jagged crest accentuated by a broad silvery flash along the tail. Both sexes become orange-yellow underneath. The larvae can become quite large and fat, with finely pointed tails, attaining at least 5-6cm before leaving the water. **Strictly protected** by British law in all its stages: it must not be disturbed or collected. The closely related **Marbled Newt** *T. marmoratus*, found southward from northern France, is very similar but basically light green with black marbling.

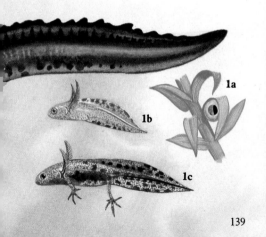

1a

1b

1c

Common or **Smooth Newt** *T. vulgaris* (**1**) is up to
11cm long. Breeding males have a prominent wavy
crest and females an inconspicuous one. Both sexes
become brighter in colour, occasionally orange
beneath. Larvae are slender with pointed tails and
rarely grow larger than 3-4cm before becoming
terrestrial (**1a**).

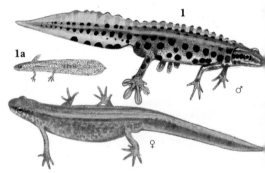

Palmate Newt *T. helveticus* (**2**) is an upland version
of the Smooth Newt but breeding males have webbed
hind feet and a delicate filament at the tip of the tail.

Alpine Newt *T. alpestris* (**3**), about 12cm long, unlike other newts, spends most of its time in water. Breeding males have a low smooth crest. Larvae resemble those of the Common Newt except for a markedly pointed tail.

3

Fire Salamander *Salamandra salamandra* (**4**), a large terrestrial newt may occasionally lay eggs in water but usually retains them in the body until they hatch; the larvae are then 'delivered' in a pond or stream (**4a**). They differ from newt larvae in their broader flatter heads, blunt tails and low crests.

4a

4

FROGS and TOADS

Frogs and toads mate and deposit their eggs (spawn) in water. Large numbers of adults may congregate in the breeding pond in the spring, calling vociferously. Males try to seize the females from behind, attaining a 'piggyback' position (**Common Toad, 1**), so that they can fertilise the spawn as it is shed by the female. Male toads become especially frantic at this time and may grab anything that appears before them, including other males or a human hand!

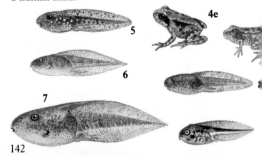

Frogs breed in early spring, typically March in Britain but varying according to the weather. Most make the familiar 'frogspawn' (**Common Frog, 4a**), a floating mass consisting of individual dark eggs, each embedded in a jelly sphere. Parsley Frogs and Tree Frogs lay individual eggs (**3**). These hatch out into the familiar tadpoles (**4b**). Their tadpoles only stay in the pond until summer – until their legs appear and develop (**4c**). When these are fully formed the tail is lost by absorption, quite rapidly over a few days, resulting in a miniature frog (**4e**) which soon leaves the water, usually during wet weather.

Toads spawn a little later than Common frogs, being very active and 'singing' frequently at this time. They produce long strings of spawn (**Common Toad 1a, Natterjack 2**), tangled around plant stems, which hatch into blackish tadpoles virtually indistinguishable from those of frogs. After breeding, toads resume a terrestrial life, not returning to water until the following spring.

Tadpoles are broadly similar but you may be able to identify **Midwife Toad (5)**, **Edible Frog (6)**, **Spadefoot Toad (7)**, **Parsley Frog (8)** and **Tree Frog (9)** in addition to the **Common Toad (1b)** and **Common Frog (4b)**.

For mature *forms of Frogs and Toads see pages 80-85.*

4c

d

1b

FISHES

Fishes are the only vertebrates that are completely adapted to life under water. In freshwater they occupy the topmost link in the food chain: most aquatic life, one way or another, ultimately becoming fish food. Fishes themselves are preyed upon by various other creatures – birds, mammals and humans.

When identifying a fish note in particular the relative position and extent along the body of the fins and the size, shape and position of the mouth and

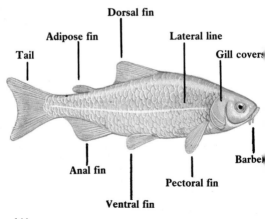

eye. The fins all have special names: dorsal, adipose, tail (or caudal fin), anal, ventral (pelvic – paired) and pectoral (paired). All fins (except the adipose) are supported, at the front edge, by one or more rigid spines, with softer flexible rays behind, but in some – the perch for instance – the dorsal fin is clearly divided into a spiny first part and a soft-rayed second.

Other points of the fish's anatomy which may help in identification are the barbels, lateral line and the gill covers.

Most freshwater fishes breed in the spring or summer. This usually involves nothing more than shedding thousands of eggs and sperms into the water and trusting the survival of the young to nature. These spawning activities are often frenzied orgies, with all caution cast to the winds, and fishes are easily approached and observed at such times.

Only a few native fishes provide any care for their young: Sticklebacks build nests and Bitterling have the odd habit of depositing eggs inside mussels.

Outside the breeding season fishes are more secretive and not often seen from above. A few that are fairly conspicuous, if present, include Trout, Pike, Carp, Rudd, Perch and Sticklebacks. In hot calm weather others – Tench, Bream and Roach – may be seen basking at the surface.

Few freshwater fishes venture into salt or even brackish water although Trout, Eels and Sticklebacks are at home in either – but, strangely, nearly all the fishes included here thrive in brackish conditions in the Baltic Sea.

TROUT FAMILY (Salmonidae)

Although predominantly fishes of fast, clear streams and rivers, trout commonly occur in still waters, either naturally or stocked by people as table or sport fishes. Wherever they live, trout are prominent fishes as they frequently feed at the surface, taking insects or chasing fish fry. Viewed from above the spots provide instant identification and members of this family also possess a small adipose fin.

Trout need clean, well-oxygenated, running water to breed in and hence rarely spawn naturally in still waters.

Brown Trout *Salmo trutta* (**1**) is an exceedingly variable species as it occurs in such a wide variety of habitats, including the sea. Typically it is darker than

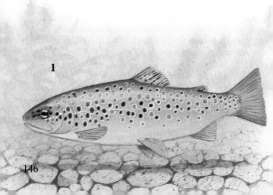

1

the Rainbow Trout (*below*) with fewer and larger spots (rarely any on the tail) some of which are usually red with a pale halo. Size also varies with habitat: in a 'poor' upland pool 15cm length may be a big fish, whereas in optimum conditions 60cm or more and a weight of 10kg is not unknown.

Rainbow Trout *S. gairdneri* (**2**), the only other common trout found in still waters, is a North American species widely used in trout farms and fisheries due to its fast growth rate. Compared to the native Browns they are typically small-headed, more silvery in colour with numerous smaller black spots, especially on the , tail, and usually have a lilac 'rainbow' stripe along the flanks.

2

EEL FAMILY (Anguillidae)

Eel *Anguilla anguilla* (**1**) is probably the most distinctive freshwater fish. It has an elongated, slippery body, lacks ventral fins and the dorsal and anal fins join on to the tail. Eels are common in most ponds but are rarely seen. They spend much time buried in mud or dense weed beds and are most active at night.

Eels must have the most amazing life history of any fish. Larval eels, odd flattened transparent creatures called **leptocephalus** (**3**), first appear in the western Atlantic's warm northeastward current (the Gulf Stream) becoming larger as they are carried eastward. Two or three years later, and by now about 6cm long, they reach European waters where they change into a more eel-like shape, but remain colourless. These **elvers** (**2**) enter river estuaries during winter and spring (February in western Britain) at last becoming pigmented. Elvers 'run' up rivers in enormous shoals, providing a rich feast for other fishes, birds and people. Survivors carry on inland until at last they

1

2

3

149

find sanctuary in some quiet pond where they grow to maturity. Eels are very hardy creatures and during wet weather can travel overland.

Mature eels, when upwards of 40cm and at least 7-10 years old, migrate back to the sea, sometimes travelling overland, eventually making their way to the western Atlantic 3000 miles away. There they spawn and presumably die.

PIKE FAMILY (Esocidae)

Pike or **Luce** *Esox lucius* (**1**) is the ultimate aquatic predator. Once it has outgrown the dangers of youth it fears little but people or otters and its diet features

any other fishes small enough to be swallowed, and even young water birds. Few fishes inspire such a sense of fascinated awe as this powerful, beautifully streamlined hunter with its calculating eye and cavernous toothy jaws. Its acceleration after its prey is sudden and startling – powered by the thrust of its tail boosted by the close-set dorsal and anal fins.

Pike spawn early in the year (February-April) so that their young are ready to feed on those of other fishes as they hatch later on. During the summer, baby pike of a few centimetres in length may often be caught in a water net from the dense weed tresses where they hide. Adolescent pike of about 30-60cm are often called jack-pike – their main preoccupation

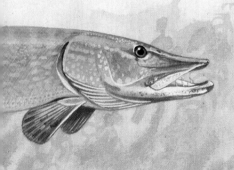

is to avoid becoming a meal for a bigger pike! In Britain pike exceptionally attain a length of 1.2m or so, weighing in excess of 20kg, but about 1m is more usual. Pike spend much time hovering or lying motionless and, with a stealthy approach, are relatively easy to observe – but all too often a great swirl is the first and last sign of a pike as it departs.

CARP FAMILY (Cyprinidae)

This is the largest and most characteristic family of freshwater fishes in Europe. All their fin-rays are soft except for the first one or two in each fin which are stiff, supporting spines. The jaws lack teeth but powerful crushing pharyngeal (throat) teeth are present. At spawning time the males usually develop small whitish pimples (tubercles) on the head and upper body – this is not a disease! Hybridisation between various species is common and the results can be most confusing, although typically inter-mediate in form between the parents. Combinations between roach, rudd and bream are the most common.

Common Carp *Cyprinus carpio* (**2**) is a magnificent, powerful fish, growing to a considerable size, 20kg or more. It is readily recognised by its long-based dorsal fin, large bronzy scales and the two barbels on its upper lip. Carp have been domesticated as table fish for centuries – they were probably introduced for this purpose, being doubtfully native in Europe.

Two variations are common. The **Leather Carp** (**3**) is devoid of scales, except for an occasional one near the fin bases. **Mirror Carp** (**1**) are usually partially scaled with huge scales in a row along the lateral line

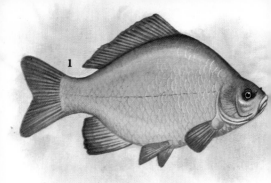

and a few around the fin bases; the occasional completely scaled mirrors are splendid creatures.

On warm calm days carp often cruise at the surface, sucking at reed stems and floating debris for anything edible – they appreciate crusts of bread – and a quiet observer can watch them easily.

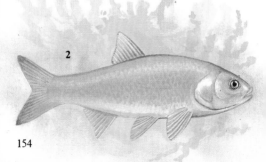

Crucian Carp *Carassius carassius* (**1**) is a chunky, very deep bodied little fish, rarely more than 25cm long. It is an inconspicuous bottom dweller in ponds throughout most of Europe.

Goldfish *C. auratus* (**3**), a more slender cousin of the Crucian Carp, is commonly released as an ornamental fish or an unwanted pet. 'Wild' goldfish, which usually revert to the natural bronzy colour, can be difficult to distinguish from crucians but are generally more slender and paler underneath, with a coarsely serrated dorsal spine (only weakly serrated in crucian).

Golden Orfe *Leuciscus idus* (**2**), a swift, slender surface dweller, and a golden variety of Tench (*see overleaf*), is one of the other 'gold' varieties of fishes sometimes introduced into ponds.

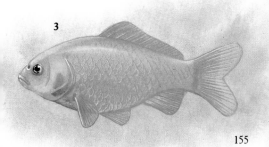

3

Tench *Tinca tinca* (**1**) is a favourite angler's fish, easily identified by its powerful slippery and slimy body, very dark dusky bronze, with tiny scales. The dark, rounded fins are also characteristic and in mature males the ventrals are thickened along the leading edge. A length of 30-40cm – about 1.5-2kg – is usual. Tench have often been raised as food fish, although slower growing than carp. In warm weather they may be seen basking at the surface and are particularly prominent when spawning (June and

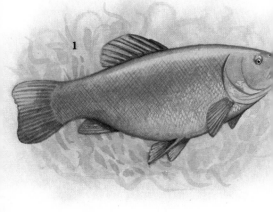

July in England) as they chase, roll and splash at the surface, causing quite a commotion. A golden variety is sometimes used as an ornamental fish.

Gudgeon *Gobio gobio* (**2**) is a friendly looking little fish, with bulging eyes and an expressive face. Two barbels protrude from the corners of the underslung mouth and the slender body, usually 10-12cm long, is attractively blotched with greeny bronze. Gudgeon are mainly found in clean rivers and streams but, as many a surprised angler has discovered, are not uncommon in ponds where the bottom is not too muddy.

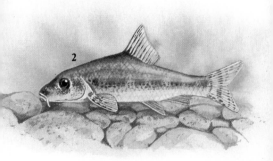

Bronze Bream *Abramis brama* (**1**) is a deep-bodied, hump-backed, very slimy fish with a long-based anal fin. Small bream, up to about 25cm long, are rather silvery but as they age they darken to deep bronze, darkest on the back. Fishes of about 2-3kg (40-45cm) are common and a very large one weighs 5-6kg. Bream are bottom feeding shoal fish, very popular with fishermen but seldom seen in the water except on hot still days when they sometimes bask at the surface. They are widely distributed in nutrient-rich ponds and sluggish lowland rivers.

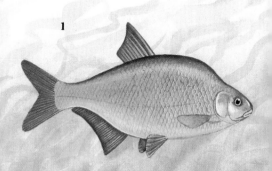

1

Silver Bream *Blicca bjoerkna* (**2**) could be mistaken for young Bronze Bream but it is more slender, more silvery-white on the flanks and rarely exceeds 25cm. The eye is relatively large, greater in diameter than its distance from the snout, whereas the opposite is true in Bronze Bream. Silver Bream are widely distributed but rather local, rare or absent in western Britain.

2

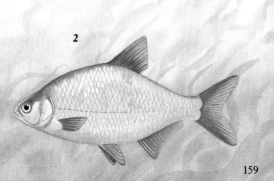

Rudd *Scardinius erythrophthalmus* (**1**) is often confused with the roach but is easily distinguished. It is deeper-bodied and more stocky, with an upturned mouth (forward opening in the roach). All its fins are red, or at least red-tinged, the eye is golden and the flanks more brassy. The base of the dorsal fin is definitely behind the ventral fin base (level in roach).

Rudd prefer slow flowing or still waters, where they are more mid-water or surface feeders than the bottom-loving roach, and hence are more likely to be seen. They occur throughout our area – including Ireland, where they are confusingly often called roach! – but are rather local.

1

Roach *Rutilus rutilus* (**2**) is probably the most popular quarry of the angler and hence one of the best known freshwater fishes. It is a handsome, nicely proportioned fish with a steely blue back, silvery flanks (often brassy in older fish), reddish pelvic and anal fins and a distinctive red eye. Typical size ranges from 10-25cm, whilst one over 40cm is enormous. Roach occur in all types of fresh waters except mountain lakes and are common throughout our area, except for Ireland, where they have been introduced.

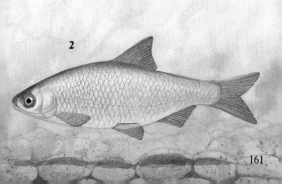

2

Bitterling *Rhodeus amarus* (**1**) is a dainty, attractive little fish, often kept in aquaria. Its fairly deep body, rarely longer than about 6cm, is silvery with a pearly iridescence, more intense in the breeding season, with a deep lilac stripe near the tail. The Bitterling inhabits quiet, clean, still waters and is widespread on the continent but not native to Britain – the current status of a small introduced population is unknown.

This fish is exceptional for its unique method of protecting its young. A ripe female grows a long tube from her vent which she inserts into a large freshwater mussel (*Anodonta* or *Unio*) where the eggs are laid. After hatching the young remain inside the mussel, being nurtured by its feeding currents, until able to fend for themselves when they exit through its siphons.

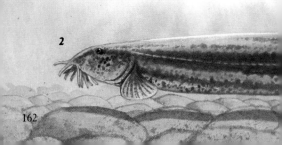

LOACH FAMILY (Cobitidae)

Pond Loach or **Weatherfish** *Misgurnus fossilis* (**2**) is easily recognised by its slippery elongated body, up to 30cm long, and eight prominent barbels. It lives in muddy pools and ditches and can tolerate foul water, using its gut as a lung to breathe swallowed air. A rarely seen bottom dweller, it becomes very active near the surface during thundery weather, thus earning its name. Although widespread on the continent it is absent from Britain.

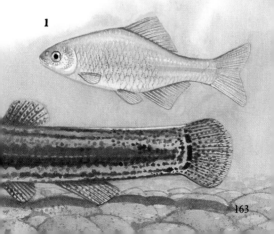

1

CATFISH FAMILY (Siluridae)

Wels or **Catfish** *Silurus glanis* (**1**) is like no other
European fish, with its broad, wide-mouthed head,
six long barbels and slimy, scale-less body. It is a
long-lived fish, capable of reaching an enormous size.
A monster of 5m and 330kg has been recorded but
1-1.5m (15-25kg) is far more usual. The Wels lives
in large ponds and slow rivers on the European
mainland and has been successfully introduced to
various lakes in Britain.

1

North American 'Bullhead' or **'Horned Pout'**
Ictalurus nebulosus (**2**) is another catfish which has
been introduced and is now frequently found in parts
of Europe, but not in Britain. It differs from the Wels
by having eight barbels and an adipose fin, and only
reaches a length of 40cm.

PERCH FAMILY (Percidae)

Perch *Perca fluviatilis* (**1**) is, at its best, a most handsome fish. The prickly first dorsal and bold stripes are instantly recognisable but the stripes may fade or merge with age. Perch are common in all kinds of freshwater, usually travelling in shoals. In small ponds they often become overcrowded and stunted, often no more than 6 or 7cm long, but given adequate space and food a perch can grow to 40cm and a weight of 2kg or more.

Perch produce distinctive strings of spawn, like miniature frogspawn but shed in lacy ribbons tangled

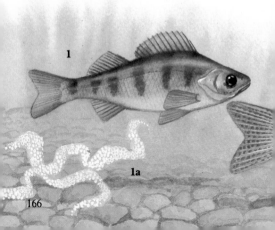

1

1a

around aquatic plants or roots (**1a**). They are popular with anglers because they take almost any bait, provided it moves, and fish of 500g or more are very tasty. Often a juvenile angler's first catch is a perch and its bristly, colourful, pugnacious appearance is usually exciting enough to 'hook' the young captor on angling for life.

Zander or **Pike-perch** *Stizostedion lucioperca* (**2**), a close relative of the Perch, is highly prized on the continent as both a sport and table fish. It is more elongated than the Perch, mottled instead of striped and attains a larger size – 50cm or more. It is an open water hunter of small fishes, widespread on the mainland and introduced to several parts of England, especially the Great Ouse system, where it is spreading.

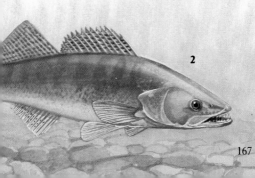

2

SUNFISHES and BASS FAMILY (Centrarchidae)
These are North American natives; they are popular
with anglers because they will readily attack an
artificial lure, fight strongly and make good eating.
Several species have been introduced into Europe,
though rarely into Britain. They are good parents,
excavating a shallow pit, in which the eggs are laid.
One or other parent will then remain on guard duty
over both eggs and young.

Large-mouthed Black Bass *Micropterus salmoides* (**1**)
reaches a size of 5kg or more in the USA but seems
limited to about 1kg (30cm or so) on this side of the

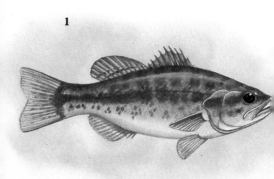

Atlantic. It is 'large-mouthed' because the bony top 'lip' reaches back as far as the hind edge of the eye and beyond, unlike the Small-mouthed Bass *M. dolomieu*, whose lip extends less far, which has been introduced on the continent of Europe but not into Britain.

Pumpkinseed Sunfish *Lepomis gibbosus* (**2**) is smaller, rarely exceeding 15cm, much deeper-bodied than the Black Basses and more colourful. It has a characteristic red (or red-edged) spot on its gill cover. This species is now fairly widespread in lowland Europe but found at only a few sites in Britain, mainly in the south.

2

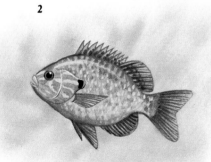

STICKLEBACK FAMILY (Gasterosteidae)

These are probably the best known freshwater fishes, a favourite quarry of small boys with toy fishing nets. Despite their small size, up to 5cm, they are not afraid to hover and dart in open water, though never far from the shelter of a weed bed, and are thus easily spotted. In these circumstances the silhouette of the spindle-shaped body, clearly narrowed near the tail, is most distinctive. Larger fishes rarely swallow sticklebacks, being easily discouraged by the strong pelvic and dorsal spines which can be locked erect. If they are seized, stickles are usually spat out with distaste.

At spawning time (spring through summer) the male selects and vigorously defends a territory within which he builds a rounded nest of plant debris. Displaying his most intense colour (**1b**) he courts an attractive female (heavy with eggs, **1a**) and lures her

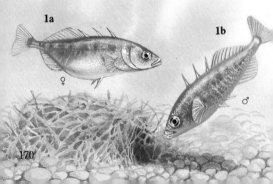

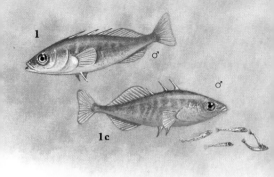

into the nest where the eggs are laid. Often more than one female is seduced in this way, afterwards being chased off. The male now asumes responsibility for the eggs, which he aerates by fanning, and later shepherds the school of baby fishes until they can fend for themselves (**1c**).

Three-spined Stickleback *Gasterosteus aculeatus* (**1**, non-breeding colours) is the commonest of our two species and is easily recognised by its two or three dorsal spines. Its colour, and the occurence of bony plates along its flanks, varies greatly according to habitat. Breeding males develop a brilliant red tummy and vivid blue eyes (**1b**). This little fish occurs in most fresh waters, still or flowing, except for upland areas, in brackish and even fully salt water in coastal regions.

Nine-spined (or **Ten-spined**) **Stickleback** *Pungitius pungitius* (**1**) is a little more slender and duller than the three-spined and bears 7-12, mostly commonly 9, dorsal spines. Breeding fishes become quite dark, males almost black, but not red beneath. They build a spherical nest near the bottom of the pond. Nine-spines are widely distributed, but more local than the other species, preferring small still or slow flowing waters with muddy bottoms and dense plant growth.

INSECTS

Many insect types have aquatic representatives, but only two – bugs and beetles – live submerged as adults. All the others are juvenile stages of terrestrial or aerial insects usually found around water (*see pages 88-107*). The adult stages are generally short-lived, whereas their aquatic young stages exist for most of the year. Details of terminology and life cycles are provided in the introduction to insects (*pages 86-7*).

MAYFLY NYMPHS

These are usually slender insects with three tails (regardless of number in the adult) and feathery or plate-like gills on the abdomen which are constantly or intermittently in motion. Most species have a life-cycle of one year, so tiny nymphs may be found during late summer or autumn, increasing in size through until late spring or summer (but *Ephemera* has a two year cycle). *For adults see page 88.*

Pond Olive *Chloeon* (**2**) nymphs are olive green or brown, often with darker mottling, up to 9mm long. Their gills are rounded plates. These are active nymphs, crawling or darting amongst weed beds and bottom debris.

2

x 3

Angler's Curse *Caenis* (**1**), compared with *Choeon* (*page 173*) has much smaller (4-8mm) relatively stout nymphs which are sluggish crawlers, often camouflaging themselves with a coat of silt. The gills are square flaps on the top of the abdomen.

Claret Dun *Leptophlebia* (**2**) nymphs are larger (12mm), dark reddish brown with gingery threadlike gills; mostly found in upland water.

Greendrake or **Mayfly** *Ephemera* (**3**) nymphs are stoutly built burrowers, 25mm long, found in gravelly mud bottoms. Handsomely marked in brown on cream, they have short, powerful, digging legs and feathery gills on top of the abdomen.

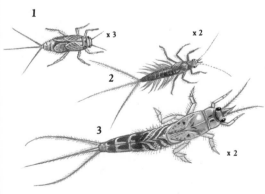

1

x 3

x 2

2

3

x 2

DRAGONFLY and DAMSELFLY NYMPHS

Dragonfly nymphs are fearsome hunters of other aquatic animals, as terrorists rating second only to the larger beetle larvae. Stout 'bug-eyed' monsters up to 5cm long, typically brownish, they are capable of swimming in short bursts by jet propulsion – water ejected forcibly backwards from a gill cavity in the abdomen providing the thrust. Typically bottom dwellers, they creep menacingly through dead leaves, mud and other debris.

Prey is captured by a unique organ, the mask (**4a**), a hinged device slung beneath the head, which can be flicked forward to seize the victim with a pair of pincers at its tip (**4b**).

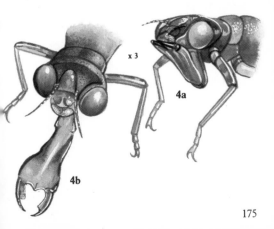

x 3

4a

4b

When fully mature the nymph crawls out of the water, often ascending plant stems. Soon the skin splits open and a complete, if somewhat crumpled dragonfly squeezes out (**Southern Hawker, 1a**). Its soft body and wings must be inflated before they harden in the air and the insect can fly away (**1b**). Nymphs of the same species frequently emerge more or less simultaneously, so probably ensuring some escape attack from insect-eating birds. Dawn or dusk are the usual times, fine weather usually being chosen.

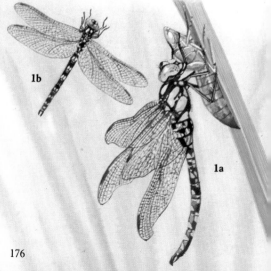

1b

1a

Hawker Dragonfly (**2**) nymphs have huge eyes, smooth cylindrical bodies and relatively short legs which do not stretch as far as the end of the body.

Darter and **Chaser Dragonfly** (**3**) nymphs have relatively small eyes and rather short, squat bodies, often hairy or silt encrusted, with long legs reaching beyond the body.

Damselfly nymphs, such as *Coenagrion* (**5**) and *Erythromma* (**4**) look rather different from those of the larger Dragonflies but their sinuous bodies, ending in three leaf-like tails, also have the characteristic mask under the head. Most inhabit the three-dimensional world of weed beds and to some extent can mimic the colour of their surroundings and so vary from green to blotchy brown. Clinging unmoving to a plant stem they are very easily to miss. They swim feebly or not at all, having no jet propulsion.

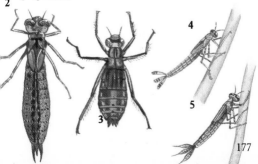

WATER BUGS (Hemiptera)

Bugs are insects whose jaws are fashioned into a long tubular snout or *rostrum*. Some resemble beetles, from which they differ in the X-shaped wing folds (compare beetles, *pages 189 ff*). Most water bugs are hunters with claw-like front legs for seizing their prey. All breathe air at the surface, retaining a store beneath their wings. Apart from Backswimmers and corixas, water bugs rarely fly at our latitudes, unless the weather is exceptionally warm. Nymphs of water bugs differ little from their parents, apart from their smaller size and lack of wings, and are easy to recognise as such. *See also page 110* Surface Bugs.

all illustrations x 1.5

1

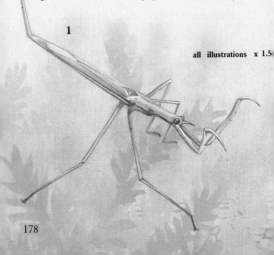

Water Scorpion *Nepa cinerea* (**2**) is a flattened brown bug, up to 23mm long plus a long breathing tube at the tail. A slow moving non-swimmer, it lurks in weed beds, where it is easily mistaken for a dead leaf, waiting to ambush any small creature (fish, tadpole or insect) that swims past.

Water Stick-insect *Ranatra linearis* (**1**) is an elongated (35mm) emaciated looking version of the water scorpion and has similar habits. Both species are most common in the southern part of our area.

Saucer Bug *Ilyocoris cimicoides* (**3**), the most beetle-like of our water bugs, is a good swimmer, 16mm long, with short, powerful, claw-like legs. Quite widespread, but mainly in the south, it should be handled cautiously as its rostrum is quite capable of piercing human flesh.

WATER BOATMEN

These all have long oar-like hind legs and are very active swimmers; their weak forelegs are used to grasp vegetation to prevent the bugs bobbing to the surface whilst resting. Adults are winged and are good fliers. Nymphs are easily recognised by their lack of wings – the top of the abdomen is visible.

Backswimmers *Notonecta* have deep boat-shaped bodies, up to 16mm long, and swim upside down. Like saucer bugs they are predators that can also bite man, but are more widespread and common. Nymphs often have a distinctive whitish 'shoulder' region. Shown are *N. maculata* (**1**) and *N. glauca* (**2**).

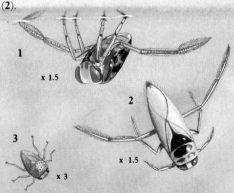

1

x 1.5

2

3

x 3

x 1.5

Lesser Backswimmers *Plea* (**3**) are tiny, only 3mm long, with a proportionately very deep body and flickering swimming motion more like water fleas than other bugs. Although common they are easily mistaken for nymphs of other boatmen unless studied closely.

Corixas or **Lesser Water Boatmen** (family Corixidae) include predatory, vegetarian and detritus feeding types. All have relatively flattened bodies, ranging from 3-15mm long according to species, and a short blunt rostrum. They swim the right way up. They are very common in all sorts of freshwater habitats and are easily discovered. *Corixa* (**4**), a large vegetarian, its nymph (**4a**), and *Cymatia* (**5**), a small predator, are shown as examples.

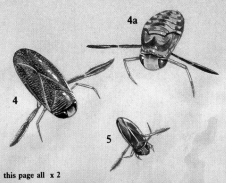

this page all x 2

ALDERFLIES and SPONGEFLIES

Alderfly *Sialis* has a distinctive, lively larva (**1**) up to 2.5cm long and common in the mud of ponds, ditches and streams. It is easily recognised by its shiny brown head and thorax and paler softer abdomen which bears straw-coloured thread-like lateral gills and a single tail. *See page 102 for adult.*

Spongefly *Sisyra* (**2**), a distant relative of the Alderfly, has a small, 5mm. larva found only on freshwater sponges (*page 231*). Sluggish, bristly, barrel-shaped and coloured green or yellow according to their sponge, they are fairly common wherever sponges occur – but they are not easy to spot. *See page 102 for adult.*

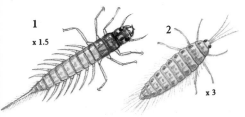

1
x 1.5

2
x 3

CADDIS LARVAE

Caddis larvae are fascinating creatures resembling caterpillars but equipped with strong legs and hence more active. Most species live in tubular mobile homes built from various materials including sand grains and plant fragments. Many have a strongly characteristic method of construction and choice of materials. Mature larvae seal off both ends of the tube before they pupate within. When perfect the adult, still inside its pupal skin, breaks out and swims to the surface to 'hatch'. (*See* Sedge Flies, *page 100-1, for the adults*)

Not all caddis build mobile tubes: some construct a large fixed tubular nest of silk and debris in which they hide and trap food. Some caddises, such as *Phryganea*, are carnivorous, others eat plants or detritus.

The following illustrations show typical cases of a selection of common caddis species. Some are less fussy about materials than others, especially *Limnephilus*, which may use anything that is available.

Great Red Sedge *Phryganea grandis* (**3**): carefully cut plant 'bricks' arranged in a neat spiral, 40mm long.

Mottled Sedge *Glyphotaelius* (**4**): large pieces of leaf enclosing a tube of smaller portions, 35mm long.

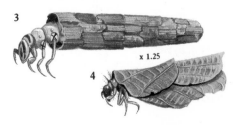

3

x 1.25

4

Brown Sedge *Limnephilus* (**1**): often consists of tiny sticks arranged crosswise, or various vegetable, mineral or even animal matter, including snail shells, sometimes with the snail still in occupation! *Molanna* (**2**): a characteristic flat, rounded plate flanges the sandy tube, 25mm long.

Silverhorns *Athripsodes, Mystacides* (**3**): slender, tapering tubes of fine sand, often curved, 25mm long. *Leptocerus* (**4**): shaped as above but made of a celluloid-like secretion, very lightweight, enabling the larvae to swim using their long paddle-like legs. *Triaenodes* (**5**): another swimmer, making a tube of leaf fragments.

Polycentropus (**6**) and others are active, green or yellowish larvae without cases. The flattish body ends in a pair of hooked claws. These larvae knit flimsy nets of silk strung amongst aquatic plants or roots (easily broken by the collector's net).

this page all x

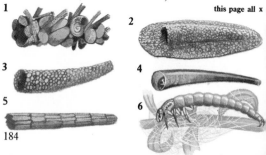

1

2

3

4

5

6

AQUATIC CATERPILLARS

China-mark Moth larvae These caterpillars are distinguished from other aquatic larvae by the five pairs of rudimentary 'prolegs' on the abdomen. Some build tubular cases like the caddis larvae and pupation takes place in this or a separate cocoon. Aquatic caterpillars are very widespread but apparently rather local. Their activities are often betrayed by the oval holes they nibble in floating leaves of lilies and other plants. *For adults see page 99.*

Nymphula nympheata (**7**) has brownish larvae which live in flattish oval cases built of water lily leaf.

Cataclysta lemnata (**8**), a very dark brown caterpillar, makes a tube out of duckweed.

Paraponyx stratiotata (**9**) is a very distinctive non-case-builder living in dense weed beds. It is up to 30mm long with branching filamentous gills.

7

this page all x 2

9

8

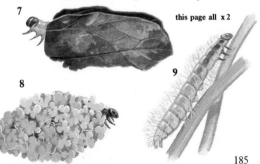

TRUE FLY LARVAE

Bloodworms These larvae, common in all standing waters from water butts to large lakes, are the young of plumed gnats (*page 104*). All species – more than 450 are known in Britain alone – share a legless segmented worm-like body shape with a well-defined head and small tail appendages. Ranging from almost microscopic to 15mm in size, most live in mud inhabiting tubes of mucus and silt (**1**), some amongst weeds, again in mucus tubes, and a few build little caddis-like cases of plant fragments or sand (**3**). Occasionally they are found swimming free with a stiff looping motion of the body (**2**).

Many of the largest species are blood-red but a huge range of colours occurs, especially green, brown or black. The big red ones are commonest in tiny stagnant water bodies because their abundance of red pigment enables them to extract what little oxygen is present.

Pupae are not unlike the larvae but have prominent wing and leg buds near the head which may also bear a tuft of fluffy white hairs (**4**). They stay in mud, pulsating gently, until ripe, when they swim jerkily to the surface to hatch. The empty pupal skins can become plentiful enough to form a strand line consisting of little else.

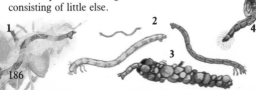

1

2

3

4

186

Mosquitoes Mosquito larvae are easily seen hanging about at the surface of water butts and other stagnant waters. They have dull greyish bodies, up to about 1cm long, with a bulbous head and a short breathing tube at the tail.

Anopheles larvae (**8**) lie horizontally, others such as ***Culex*** (**6**) at an angle to the surface, to breathe the air above. When alarmed they wriggle into the depths to escape. Their pupae have similar habits but are like wriggly commas (**7**). Where mosquitos breed regularly it is not difficult to find the neat little egg rafts floating on the surface (**5**).

Phantom Larvae *Chaoborus* (**9**) is another frequent inhabitant of small waters whose adult stage is difficult to distinguish from a plumed gnat. A transparent larvae, about 1cm long, and almost invisible but for the fore and aft air sacs which allow it to hang motionless in mid water, though it also swims rapidly in short spurts. Unlike other midge larvae, which filter tiny food particles from the water, this is a hunter, capturing small prey such as water fleas with its fang-like mouthparts. Pupae resemble those of mosquitos but possess 'ears' (**10**)

all illustrations x 2

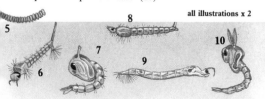

Biting Midges have larvae in a variety of shapes and not always aquatic. The commonest type is ***Culicoides*** (**1**), a stiffly jointed, colourless worm up to 1cm long, found amongst debris or dense masses of algae.

Crane-fly or **Daddy-long-legs** *Tipula* larvae (**2**) sometimes breed in water, although usually in damp soil. A large, 3cm, greyish maggot-like creature it can occasionally be found among the mud and detritus near pond edges.

Horse Flies *Tabanus* produce predatory larvae which are often found in bogs or woodland pools. Maggots (**3**), up to 2cm long, they can be distinguished by their pointed heads and rings of wart-like 'pro-legs' around the body.

Rat-tailed Maggot *Eristalis* (**4**) must be the most bizarre fly larva. Found in small temporary pools, tree holes and the like, it survives in foul water by breathing air through the amazing telescopic snorkel extending from its tail. After forming a pupa in damp soil or dead leaves it emerges as a large bee-mimicking hover-fly.

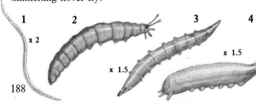

1 **2** **3** **4**

x 2

x 1.5

x 1.5

WATER BEETLES (Coleoptera)

Together with water bugs (*pages 178-81*), these are the only insects with habitually aquatic adults. Beetles have pincer-like biting jaws and their forewings form rigid cases or *elytra*, guarding the hind wings folded beneath. The plate between elytra and head is called the *pronotum*. The larvae are also aquatic and vary from fat sedentary grubs to fierce active hunters. Most come out of the water to pupate in damp soil or crevices but some stay submerged. Adult beetles range from slow crawlers to active swimmers. All are very buoyant due to the air, collected at the surface, which is stored beneath the elytra or on the hairy underside.

Whirligig Beetles *Gyrinus* (**5**), although less than 8mm long, are probably the most conspicuous water beetles as they spend much of their time at the surface, especially in warm calm weather when most human observers tend to be about. They are rapid swimmers beneath or on the surface, where they trail a conspicuous wake (*page 111*). Their eyes are divided at the waterline for simultaneous vision above and beneath the surface. The larvae (**5a**) bear a vague resemblance to sluggish centipedes and, although voracious predators, are rather secretive, hiding amongst detritus or vegetation in shallow water.

5

5a

x 2

Haliplus (**1**) includes several species having no common name. They are small (3-5mm) beetles very common in many still water habitats, especially small weedy ponds. The arched, streamlined body is brassy yellow, striped or blotched with darker brown. Although not especially designed for swimming, these beetles can scurry briskly through the water. The cylindrical larvae (**1a**) are distinctive crawlers, commonly found in thickets of filamentous algae or other plant life.

Squeak or **Screech Beetle** *Hygrobia hermanni* (**2**) is a 8-10mm beetle that often identifies itself by producing a loud rasping noise when removed from the water. Its handsome copper and black body is deeply keeled and the beetle swims well with alternate strokes of its legs.

The larva (**2a**), in its black and gold livery, is even more striking than the adult, though silent. It bulldozes its way through mud and detritus in small muddy ponds, nosing out the *Tubifex* and other worms on which it feeds.

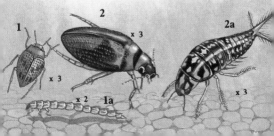

1
x 3

2
x 3

2a
x 3

x 2   1a

Noterus **Beetles** (**4**) are about 5mm long with brassy bodies, smoothly curved above but almost flat beneath. The larvae are rarely seen, spending their lives buried in the mud.

DIVING BEETLES (Dytiscidae)

This is a large family of several hundred species, ranging from a mere 1.5mm to giants of nearly 4cm. They are powerful streamlined swimmers, 'rowing' with their oar-like back legs working in unison. Air is stored beneath the elytra and regularly changed at the surface via the tail end.

Great Diving Beetles *Dytiscus* are easily the largest. **D. marginalis** (**3**) is up to 38mm and is the most common. It is yellowish below with a yellow

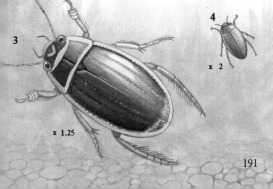

3

4

x 2

x 1.25

margin all round the pronotum. **_D. semisulcatus_ (1)** is almost as common and a little smaller, about 30mm, blackish below with only the lateral margins of the pronotum yellow.

These beetles are all fierce predators. Their larvae (**1a**), up to 60mm long, are the 'top' invertebrate predators of freshwater, tackling almost anything that moves. They are manoeuvrable swimmers with savage pincer-like jaws. Adult beetles are capable of taking prey larger than themselves (earthworms, small fishes, tadpoles, etc) but mostly being content with smaller insects and crustaceans. Males can be told from females by their curiously shaped forelegs and smooth elytra (grooved in females). With the few exceptions noted below all other diving beetle larvae are similar but smaller.

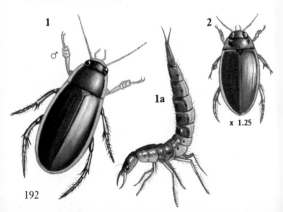

x 1.25

Acilius sulcatus (5) is next in size, about 15-18mm long. It is a flattish pear-shaped beetle with dusky mottled elytra; males and females differ as in *Dytiscus*. Its larvae **(5a)** have a distinctive long 'neck' (pronotum).

Colymbetes fuscus (2) is similar in size to *Acilius* but less heavily built. The elytra appear greyish but on close inspection can be seen to be dull yellow with numerous very fine blackish crosswise lines.

Ilybius ater (3) is wholly blackish and up to 15mm long. Its smaller relative **I. fuliginosus (4)** is blackish brown with dull yellowish outer edges to its elytra.

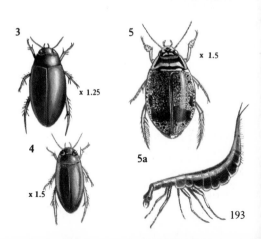

3

x 1.25

5

x 1.5

4

x 1.5

5a

Agabus bipustulosus (**1**) is also about 11mm long, dull blackish all over, sometimes with two faint reddish spots between the eyes. ***A. nebulosus*** (**2**), another common *Agabus* of a different type, is smaller (8-9mm) and pale grey-brown with a dark head and mottling on the elytra.

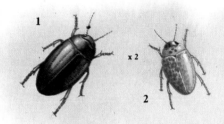

TINY DIVING BEETLES
There are numerous species of tiny diving beetles, mostly less than 5mm long and difficult to identify. The four species following are fairly distinct and very widespread. Their larvae differ from the larger types by possessing an elongated snout.

Hydroporus palustris (**3**), 3.5mm, is black with a yellow pattern.

Graptodytes pictus (**4**) is a tiny, 2-2.5mm, broad-bodied beetle, reddish brown with a yellowish pattern on the elytra.

Hygrotus inaequalis (**5**), is a tubby, 3mm beetle, strongly convex above *and* below. Head and pronotum are reddish, elytra are black with reddish mottling.

Hyphydrus ovatus (**6**), 5mm, has the fattest body of all, as deep as it is wide, orange-red with darker markings. Its black and yellow banded larva (**6a**) is most distinctive.

this page all x 3

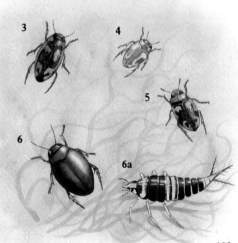

195

HYDROPHILIIDAE

This is the largest family after the Diving Beetles and occurs in a similar range of sizes. The beetles differ in being weak or non-swimmers and they collect air at the surface via their antennae, which are short and curiously adapted for this purpose. Air thus obtained is stored as a silvery bubble against the furry belly. These beetles are mostly inhabitants of small weedy ponds, which they leave readily in warm weather to fly. The larvae are slow-moving (having very weak legs), soft-bodied but often with large jaws. Some are predatory whilst others feed on detritus.

Great Silver Beetle *Hydrophilus piceus* (**2**), at 4cm or more long, is the largest species of the family and one of the largest beetles – also, sadly, one of the rarest – in Britain. In the past it has been a popular subject for aquaria and insect collectors, and this, together with loss of many habitats, has led to its near extinction in Britain, though it is still frequent on the continent. Despite its name (referring to the air bubble) it is black with a green sheen. Its larva (**2a**) is a huge (6cm) predator of snails, which it prises open with its strong jaws.

Hydrobius fuscipes (**1**) is a much smaller, 6-8mm, version of the Great Silver Beetle and is also one of the commonest of this family. Apart from size and its slightly reddish legs there is scarcely any difference between this species and *H. piceus*. The fat larva (**1a**) is found in dense vegetation, especially rafts of filamentous algae.

196

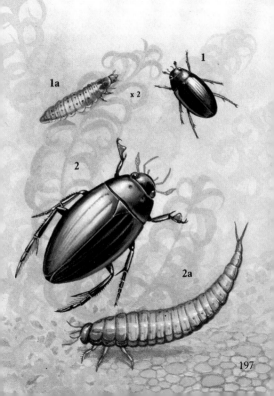

1a   x 2   1

2

2a

Helophorus (**1**) is a large genus of distinctive and attractive beetles, many species being common and closely similar. The head and deeply grooved pronotum are metallic coppery bronze whilst the elytra are metallic green-gold with rows of dark pinpricks.

Laccobius (**2**) is another genus that includes many similar species, all about 3-4mm long and almost indistinguishable to the eye. Their dark patterned heads, patterned pronotum and yellowish elytra, bearing rows of tiny pinpricks, occasionally with darker blotches, are characteristic.

Helochares species (**3**) are orange or reddish beetles, 5-6mm long, widespread but rather local. The female has the unusual habit of carrying her eggs in a disc-shaped mass slung beneath her abdomen.

HELODIDAE

This beetle family (also called Scirtidae) is terrestrial but its larvae (**4**) are often aquatic and live amongst dead leaves or exposed roots in shallow edges or temporary pools. They are flattened, well-armoured, up to 10mm long, with small but strong legs and characteristic long beaded antennae. A tiny bunch of fluffy white gills can be protruded from the tail.

CHRYSOMELIDAE

This family of leaf beetles includes **Donacia** (*adult page 103*) one of the few terrestrial beetles with aquatic larvae. The fat whitish grub (**5**) is found loosely attached to the roots of aquatic plants such as Burr-reed and Waterlily. It can breathe air from the plant's tissues, using a pair of hollow spikes inserted into the stem. The brownish pupal cocoon (**5a**) may also be found below water attached to the same stems.

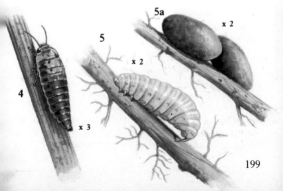

5a

x 2

5

x 2

4

x 3

SPIDERS and MITES (Arachnida)

Spiders and their relatives differ from insects by having eight legs, a body divided into only two regions – abdomen and head/thorax unit – and lacking wings.

Water Spider *Argyroneta aquatica* (**1**) used to be common in ponds, ditches and marshes, amongst dense vegetation, but is now rather local, probably due to collecting for aquaria. It is the only spider in Europe which lives underwater, where it inhabits an air-balloon-like nest consisting of a large silvery air bubble contained in a silken web (**1a**). Air is carried from the surface to the nest as a glistening layer stuck in the fine hairs of the spider's furry abdomen and brushed into the nest from below. The male (size up to 16mm) and smaller female (11mm) normally live in separate nests and the eggs are laid in that of the female. Like most spiders these are voracious hunters, preying on any small aquatic animals that they can catch.

Water Mites are related to spiders but are much smaller. During the warmer months they can be extremely common in ponds, either free swimming or crawling in weed beds or on the bottom. They prey on tiny animals, such as water fleas, which are seized in the jaws and sucked dry of body fluids through a tubular proboscis. Identification of water mites is very difficult. In ponds the most prominent are large red ones (**2**) – up to 6 or 7mm – but there are many others that are duller, smaller and less conspicuous – green, grey, yellowish and generally about 0.5-2mm.

Eggs are laid in a small blob of jelly attached to water plants or stones. Larval mites hatch from these; they have only six legs, huge jaws, and are often bright orange. They attach themselves to other animals, mainly insects, living as blood-sucking parasites. Eventually they drop off and undergo a resting stage similar to the insect pupa, usually overwintering like this before a final change into adult form.

all illustrations x 3

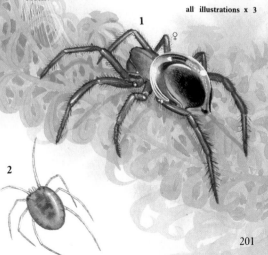

1

♀

2

CRUSTACEA

These animals have a body structure similar to that of insects and spiders – with an hardened jointed 'skin' – but are mostly aquatic (woodlice being an exception) and usually possess more than four pairs of legs. Females of most species carry their eggs until they hatch, either attached to certain legs or in a special brood pouch.

WATER FLEAS

Numerous species of these tiny crustaceans, belonging to two very different groups, live a free-swimming existence as plankton in freshwaters. Their jerky swimming actions and small size – from less then 1 to 3 or 4mm – has resulted in the general name water flea. A few sweeps of a fine-meshed net will usually produce plenty of examples.

Cladocera (often called 'daphnia' after the most common genus) have a distinctive shape (**1**) due to a large folded plate (carapace) attached to the head, which enfolds the rest of the body, including the legs, leaving free only the long forked antennae, used for swimming. Colours range from translucent greenish to brown or red. Dense swarms of daphnia can discolour the water. Many aquarists consider them to be the supreme food for their fishes.

Most species are commonest during the warmer months, when females usually produce eggs without being fertilised by males (a process called *partheno-*

genesis), which allows more rapid reproduction in times of plenty. In autumn males appear (they are rare or absent in summer) and the fertilised females produce 'winter eggs' which persist through the cold period, sometimes enclosed in a pouch (ephippium) originating from the carapace of the now dead parent. These hatch in spring.

Copepoda differ greatly from daphnia in both shape and movement. They lack a carapace and swim either slowly and precisely, using the legs, or dart rapidly by flicking their long antennae. Both sexes are common and ripe females are easily identified by the pair of egg sacs slung like saddle-bags from the abdomen.

Cyclops (**2**),　the most common genus, occurs throughout the year and is likely to turn up in most unlikely places – treeholes, puddles and other small pieces of water as well as in ponds. A related genus, ***Diaptomus*** (**3**) has even longer antennae and only a single, centrally mounted egg sac.

all illustrations x 7

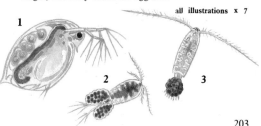

SHRIMPS (Amphipoda)

Most members of this group are rather similar in form, with groups of legs variously modified for grasping, walking and swimming.

Freshwater Shrimp *Gammarus pulex* (**1**) is well-known and found in rivers, lakes and stream-fed ponds, where it feeds on various types of detritus, from rotting leaves to dead animals.

Gammarus needs well-oxygenated water and until recently most small ponds (typically poor in oxygen) were shrimpless. But around 1936 a 'new' shrimp appeared: ***Crangonyx pseudogracilis*** (**2**). This North American species, probably accidentally introduced with water plants, appeared in London and has since spread through most of Britain (but not the continent) occupying the vacant niche of 'small pond shrimp'.

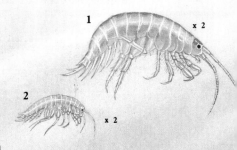

With practice the two are easily distinguished. *Gammarus* is often more than 10m long and varies from translucent olive to ginger or grey; *Crangonyx* is less than 9mm, more opaque and usually dark steely grey. If placed in a clean dish *Gammarus* tends to shuffle along on its side, whereas *Crangonyx* tends to walk upright. Because of their very different requirements these shrimps are rarely found in the same place.

Fairy Shrimps *Chirocephalus* (**3**) are rare and beautiful creatures, up to 35mm long, found only in temporary pools in woodland or ancient forests. They cruise around slowly, upside down, using the graceful rippling motion of their numerous limbs for swimming and also for filtering out microscopic algae for food. Their eggs are very hardy, resistant to drying or freezing, so although the adults die when their pond dries out a new generation hatches when the water returns.

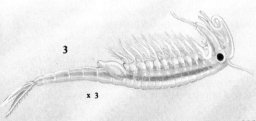

3

x 3

SEED SHRIMPS (Ostracoda)

These are tiny – less than 1mm to over 4mm – very abundant crustaceans (**1**) with a 'shell' (carapace) consisting of two halves hinged together, like a mussel, covering the entire body. They scuttle about, rarely swimming, over plants or bottom debris, only the tips of their legs and antennae protruding from the shell opening which is clamped shut if the animal takes fright.

1

x 5

FISH LICE (Branchiura)

Fish Louse *Argulus* (**2**) is a common parasite living on the skin or fins of various fishes, sucking the blood. It has a flattened, well camouflaged body, up to 10mm long, equipped with a pair of circular suckers with which it clamps on to its host, aided by the hooked front legs. The posterior four pairs of legs are used for swimming and as gills, beating constantly. It is a suprisingly good swimmer, gliding over its host in a ghostly manner, or moving from fish to fish. Unlike most crustaceans *Argulus* deposits its eggs in a small mass of jelly stuck to a stone or plant stem. The commonest hosts are probably sticklebacks and pike.

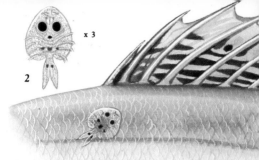

x 3

2

WATER LICE (Isopoda)

Water Louse *Asellus aquaticus* (**3**), also called Hog Louse or Water Slater, is easily recognised as an aquatic version of the familiar woodlouse, differing only in its more flattened body, up to 15mm long, and longer legs. Water lice are common in nearly all aquatic habitats where they feed on decaying plant material and other detritus. They cannot swim but scramble about actively in the open despite the fact that they are preyed upon by other creatures, especially the flatworm *Dendrocoelum* and dragonfly nymphs.

3

x 2

CRAYFISHES (Decapoda)

Crayfishes are unmistakable freshwater lobsters, living under stones or in holes under banks. They are characteristic of clean, well-oxygenated running water but occasionally live and breed in ponds, especially stream-fed ones. Unfortunately for crayfishes they are very good to eat and over the years other species, mainly from North America, have been introduced in attempts at commercial farming. The American species carry a fungal disease, to which they are immune, which has infected and wiped out many native populations which have no natural resistance. With more alien crayfish being imported, to grow as a bonus crop on trout farms, our native species is disappearing from many rivers at an alarming rate, especially in the south.

Austropotamobius pallipes (**1**) is the native species in Britain and lowland Europe, up to 12cm long and yellowish brown. *Astacus astacus*, 15cm and reddish brown, also occurs on the continent. Signal Crayfish *Pacifastacus lenuisculus*, the most commonly introduced species, is up to 15cm long and reddish brown with a white signal flash on the hinge of the claw.

1

MOLLUSCS

The two groups of molluscs occurring in freshwater – Snails (*below*) and Mussels (*page 216*) – are so different that they are introduced separately.

SNAILS and LIMPETS (Gastropoda)

Freshwater snails are common and easily recognised animals. Most have a coiled shell raised into a spire (**2**), but Ramshorns (**3**) and the Flat Valve Snail have flattish shells without a spire, and limpets (**4**) have simple uncoiled cones. Nearly all freshwater shells are *dextral* – the aperture is on the right when viewed frontally, as in (**2**) – but Bladder snails coil the other way and hence are *sinistral* (**5**).

Many species are very widely distributed and favourable habitats, especially weedy lowland ponds, can contain as many as 20 species! The main factor controlling distribution is water quality. Most snails require hard, lime-rich water. Only a few can tolerate soft (usually acidic) waters, such as peaty upland ponds and streams – these are indicated in the text by * beside their names. Those tolerant of soft waters may occur in any water, including hard conditions; none is exclusive to soft water.

Snails usually graze the film of algae and fine detritus that forms constantly on every surface, using their sandpaper-like tongues (*radulae*) to scrape it off. A few will feed on dead animal matter when this is available.

Water snails divide into two groups – operculates and pulmonates. *Operculates* are snails which, on retreating into their shells, seal the aperture with a circular lid or *operculum* (*see* **2**, **3**, **5** *on page 209*); they also breathe using gills. *Pulmonates* are snails without an operculum; breathing air at the surface using a kind of lung.

OPERCULATES

Nerite *Theodoxus fluviatilis* (**3**) has an unmistakeable thick shell, 12mm long, with a large D-shaped aperture. Though normally an inhabitant of running water, it occasionally turns up in canals and ponds, especially those connected to rivers. Eggs are deposited in individual horny capsules.

River Snails *Viviparus*, despite their name, are frequent in still waters. Easily the largest freshwater snails, up to 40cm, their shells have broad dark bands and young snails (**1a**) are hairy! *V. viviparus* (**2**) has a matt shell with shallow grooves; *V. fasciatus* (**1**), less common, has a glossy, deeply grooved shell. Both species produce live young.

★ **Valve Snails** *Valvata* have two common species. Both have a preference for running water but may be found in ponds and ditches. They deposit several eggs in a spherical capsule of horn-like material about 1mm diameter. **Common Valve Snail** *V. piscinalis* (**4**) is largest, up to 7mm high and wide. **Flat Valve Snail** *V. cristata*, with a flat-coiled shell only 4mm across, resembles Ramshorns (*page 215*) but has an operculum.

★ **Jenkins' Snail** *Potamopyrgus* (or *Hydrobia*) *jenkinsi* (**5**) is another small operculate that prefers rivers but is sometimes found in still waters, often in huge numbers. The shell, usually less than 5mm tall, is pale brown but usually encrusted with a dark deposit. Living young are produced.

This snail has an interesting history, having successfully 'invaded' freshwater since the turn of the century, previously being a brackish salt-marsh inhabitant. It is now widespread in freshwaters in many parts of Britain and Europe.

Bithynia, although perhaps the commonest genus of operculate snail, has no common name. **B. tentaculata** (**6**) is largest, up to 15mm tall, with shallow shell grooves. *B. leachii* never exceeds 8mm and has deeper grooves. It is more local than *tentaculata*. Eggs are laid in transparent capsules forming a neat double row.

x 3

6

211

PULMONATES

All species lay their eggs (from few to many) enclosed in a blob of firm clear jelly stuck to plants or stones (**1a**).

* **Dwarf Pond Snail** *Lymnaea truncatula* (**4**) is usually only 6mm tall or less, but can reach 12mm. The spire is blunt and the aperture equals about half the total height. This little snail inhabits ponds and ditches but is most at home in moist water meadows or drying mud around ponds. It has great economic importance to man as it carries the infective stage of liver fluke, a nasty parasitic disease of sheep and cattle and occasionally of man.

* **Marsh Snail** *L. palustris* (**3**) is similar to *truncatula* but larger, commonly 15mm but up to 30mm, more slender and sharply pointed. The shell surface often bears raised criss-cross lines and/or a blackish encrustation. This snail often occurs in damp places out of water, being characteristic of ponds and ditches which dry up in summer.

Great Pond Snail *L. stagnalis* (**1**) is a very well known and common species. Its shell, up to 50mm tall, has a sharply pointed spire and a seemingly huge aperture, although this is only about half the height. Due to its great size, this snail is usually one of the first to be discovered, especially as in warm weather it spends much time near the surface.

* **Wandering Snail** *L. peregra* (**5**) is the most widespread and abundant of all water snails. Its shape is rather

variable but the aperture is always more than three-quarters of the total shell height, which is up to 25mm. This species can be found from high mountain streams to muddy lowland ponds, in large lakes or fast rivers.

Ear Snail *L. auricularia* (**2**) is similar to *peregra* but is larger, up to 35mm, has a very widely flared aperture and an inconspicuous but very sharp spire. Ear snails are not uncommon but never seem to occur in large numbers where they are found.

* **Bladder Snails** *Physa* are common little animals with fragile bulbous shells which are sinistral. When the snail is 'out' and active the shell is partly covered by finger-like folds of flesh which create a highly polished surface.

Physa fontinalis (**6**) is probably the only native species, up to 12mm long, with a very short spire. Other species which are sometimes found, such as *P. acuta* (up to 18mm with a more prominent spire) are thought to be aliens, probably introduced with aquarium plants.

213

* **Moss Bladder Snail** *Aplexa hypnorum* (**1**) is another sinistral species, having a slender tapering shell up to 12mm tall. The flesh of the body is almost black and does not wrap around the outside of the shell as in *Physa*. Moss Bladder snails occur in temporary ponds and ditches which dry up in summer.

Ramshorn Snails, *Planorbis* and others, are easily recognised by their more or less flat-coiled shells which are never raised into a spire. Many species are common in the area, distinguished by the number of visible coils, shape of the aperture and general size and proportions. Only the common species are given here and in a good pond it would not be a great surprise to find them all.

Great Ramshorn *Planorbarius corneus* (**2**) is easily the biggest, typically 20-25mm diameter and 8-10mm thick, but it can reach 35 x 12mm.

Common Ramshorn *Planorbis planorbis* (**3**) is medium sized, up to 18 x 4mm, with a small raised ridge (*keel*) around its outer edge.

2   3   all x 1.25   4

214

Keeled Ramshorn *P. carinatus* (**4**) is similar to the Common, but has a larger aperture with a squashed shape and a prominent keel.

Whirlpool Ramshorn *P. vortex* (**5**) has a slender shell, about 10 x 2mm, with numerous visible coils (usually six to eight). A slight keel is sometimes present.

★ **Button Ramshorn** *P. leucostoma* (**6**) is very similar to the Whirlpool but has a more rounded aperture and never a hint of a keel.

★ **White Ramshorn** *P. albus* (**7**) resembles the Great Ramshorn in shape but is much smaller, about 8 x 2.5mm. The shell is often whitish, but can be brown, and usually bears raised concentric lines.

★ *P. contortus* (**8**) has a very distinctive shape, the narrow coils and slit–like aperture form a shell whose depth is about half its diameter, to 6 x 3mm.

★ **Flat Ramshorn** *Segmentina complanata* (**9**) is another small but easily recognised species, up to 6 x 2mm, with wide flattish coils producing a distinctly lens-shaped shell.

this page all x 2

5   6   7

8   9

Freshwater Limpets share a similar lifestyle with their marine namesakes but are only distantly related. They graze over smooth firm surfaces, such as stones or reed stems, where they can clamp their shells down tightly if threateneed. There are two species.

Lake Limpet *Acroloxus lacustris* (**1**) is commonest in still water. Its shell is up to 7 x 4mm but its height, to the tip of the cone, is always less than the width.

River Limpet *Ancylus fluviatilis* (**2**) lives in running waters and larger ponds. Its thicker shell reaches 8 x 6mm and is about as tall as wide.

x 5

MUSSELS (Bivalvia)
Mussel shells form two matching halves, hinged together at the dorsal edge, which clamp shut when the animal is worried. Suprisingly, mussels are quite mobile, levering themselves around with a fleshy muscular foot (**3a**). They feed by drawing in water through a tubular *siphon* (**3b**), filtering out the edible particles (microscopic plankton and detritus) then expelling it through another siphon. This flow of water

also supplies oxygen and disposes of waste. Most of the space inside the shell is taken up by the filtering apparatus of curtain-like gills. Mussels have no head or eyes.

Zebra Mussel *Dreissena polymorpha* (**4**), up to 4cm long, is most like the edible marine mussel that stars in the dish *moules marinière*. Clean specimens are strikingly marked with black and white zig-zag lines, but these are often worn away or overgrown by algae. This mussel can attach itself to other objects using tough silky guy ropes called *byssus* threads, which can be severed if the mussel wants to move somewhere else. It breeds by releasing thousands of tiny larvae that swim away to settle elsewhere and change into baby mussels. Unlike other freshwater mussels this one does not burrow but attaches itself to firm surfaces – rocks, sunken branches or masonry, etc – often forming extensive colonies in canals and lakes.

Anodonta and ***Unio*** mussels live partly buried in soft sediments with only the siphons and adjacent corners of the shell protruding (**1**). Dead shells are commonly found in dredging spoil or amongst debris in shallow waters.

Young mussels of this group have evolved an ingenious trick to achieve wide dispersal – the parents do not move around very much. Larvae are brooded inside the parent for a time, developing into strange, toothed creatures called *glochidia* (**2**), which are expelled in great numbers in the spring. Once free, they must catch a fish, using a long sticky thread, and then staple themselves to its skin or fins (**2a**), where a cyst is formed around them. After two to four weeks, depending on the temperature, the encysted larvae have transformed into tiny mussels. They then work their way out of the cyst and drop to the bottom to live, by now perhaps miles away from their parents.

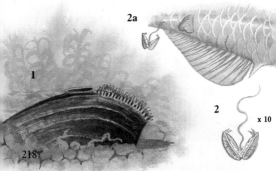

2a

1

2

x 10

this page all x 0.5

Swan Mussel *Anodonta cygnea* (**4**) is the largest species. The shell is up to 15cm long and dull coloured – olive or brownish, often with blackish stains – on the outside, but its inner surface is the lovely iridescent mother-of-pearl once used to make pearl buttons and other trinkets. Swan mussels are widespread in lowland ponds, canals and slow rivers, wherever there is a firm (not 'gloopy') muddy bottom.

A less common and more local species *A. complanata* (**5**) is sometimes found in canals and rivers. Its shell is broader and more wedge-shaped than *cygnea* and rarely exceeds 9cm.

Painters' Mussel *Unio pictorum* (**3**), up to 10cm, has a much more swollen shape with a blunt angle where the shell edges meet rather than the sharp-edge of *Anodonta*. It is common in canals and lakes having a firm muddy bottom.

Freshwater 'Cockles' *Sphaerium* (**1**) and **Pea Mussels** *Pisidium* (**2**) are two very common and widespread genera containing many rather similar species. They have yellowish rounded shells up to 15mm in *Sphaerium* and usually no more than 5mm in *Pisidium* (but one species reaches 12mm). *Sphaerium* has long separate siphon tubes whereas *Pisidium* has short tubes joined together. These mussels can be found in a huge variety of habitats, sometimes burrowing into sediments or living between particles of gravel, or even climbing amongst plantlife using a ladder of mucus. They brood their few young internally until they have developed into miniature mussels which are then released.

this page x 3

1

2

WORMS and LEECHES (Annelida)

This group includes the familiar earthworms and sinister leeches. They are characterised by the elongated body being divided into numerous narrow segments. Most of the freshwater species lay their eggs in cocoons of hornlike material, from which hatch tiny replicas of the parents. Some, such as

Tubifex, can also regenerate new worms from broken fragments.

EARTHWORMS and relatives (Oligochaeta)
Ordinary earthworms are frequently washed into ponds, where they drown if not snapped up by a fish, but several species live under water, being found in mud amongst the roots of marginal plants or under stones.

Square-tailed Worm *Eiseniella tetraedra* (**3**) is quite common and widespread. It is up to 8cm long, 'earthworm' pink to brownish and distinguished by the rear half of its body being distinctly square in section.

Sparganophilus tamesis (**4**), rather locally distributed, is larger, up to 20cm, and circular in section throughout its length. Its pale bluish-pink body is firm and muscular to the touch and bears a greenish sheen.

Mud worms *Tubifex* (**1**) This large group of similar species are well known to aquarists as they are sold by pet shops as a live food for tropical fishes. These sinuous worms are up to 5cm long but only about 1mm thick; cleaned of mud they tend to coil together to form a writhing ball (**1a**). Their translucent blood red colour is due to a blood pigment which helps them to extract oxygen from the water with great efficiency, enabling them to live in badly polluted waters. *Tubifex* live buried head first in bottom muds, constructing a flimsy mud tube from which the tail end protrudes (**1b**), acting as a kind of gill by being waved to and fro in the water, but hastily withdrawn if alarmed. The massed tails of a dense worm bed can lay a red carpet across the bottom of a pond. Such densities are frequently found in shallow 'cattle drinks' in late summer, once the crop of animal droppings has 'ripened' the water; at other times numbers are much smaller.

1a

1b

x 2

LEECHES (Hirudinea)

Despite the revulsion that they inspire in many people, leeches are merely rather muscular, very elastic worms with a sucker (for attachment) at each end. Some eat small animals whole, others suck blood or body fluids of a variety of animals, but the only human bloodsucker in our territory is extremely rare. Leeches move about by looping (2) and some can swim with a graceful undulating motion. They also spend a great deal of time resting, attached to some solid object such as a stone or reed stem. Eggs are laid in hard cocoons attached to similar surfaces and fully formed young leeches eventually hatch out. One species, *Glossiphia heteroclita*, carries eggs and young beneath its body. Lengths given here are for leeches at rest, extended ones can become much larger.

2

Fish Leech *Piscicola geometra* (**3**) is an active, slender, wiry leech about 1-5cm long with prominent suckers. It sucks the blood of fishes by inserting its proboscis, through the front sucker, into soft tissues of the fish unprotected by scales (fin bases, gills, inside the mouth). When hungry it lurks in ambush, body extended, waiting for a victim to pass within range of its front sucker. Having clamped on to the fish it moves about freely on its skin until it finds a place to dine. This leech is a good swimmer frequenting large ponds.

3   x 2

this page all x 1.5

Hemiclepsis marginata (1) feeds on fishes or amphibians. It is only about 2cm long and strongly flattened, unlike the cylindrical *Piscicola*, with a striking chequered pattern. This non-swimming species is common in small ponds.

Theromyzon tessulatum (2) is very soft bodied, almost jelly-like, up to 3cm long and a non-swimmer. It is a blood sucker of waterfowl, especially ducks, attacking the soft parts around the head and even entering the nostrils or mouth. After feeding it becomes disgustingly bloated and may rest for weeks digesting its meal.

Glossiphonia and **Helobdella** are broad bodied, strongly flattened leeches which suck the body fluids of many small invertebrates, particularly snails. They are inactive non-swimmers, very common under stones or in similar leechy hideaways.

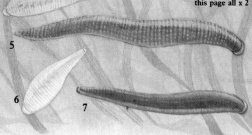

G.complanata (**3**) is up to 3cm long, green with brown markings, its upper surface rough and pimply.

G. heteroclita (**4**), 1.5cm, is translucent amber, smooth above.

Helobdella stagnalis (**6**), 12mm long, translucent pale grey or cream, has a tiny hard scale on its back (a magnifying glass is needed to see this).

Erpobdella species are brown, nearly cylindrical leeches with indistinct front suckers. They feed on small invertebrates (especially insect larvae) which are swallowed whole. They are good swimmers and may also burrow into mud or gravel.

E. octoculata (**5**) is up to 4cm long and usually patterned with blackish marking. *E. testacea* (**7**) is about 3cm long and plain brown.

225

Horse Leech *Haemopis sanguisuga* (**1**) probably derives it name from Old English (*horse* = coarse or large) referring to its size, up to 6cm – it does not suck the blood of horses! The stout, slightly flattened body is dark olive to blackish above with a pale lateral stripe. Horse leeches are locally distributed in ponds or marshes, sometimes under stones just above water level, usually in unspoilt countryside, where they feed on any small animal (up to the size of a young frog) which can be swallowed whole.

Medicinal Leech *Hirudo medicinalis* (**2**) resembles (1) in size and shape but is more richly patterned with tapestry-like markings of red, yellow and black. It sucks the blood of mammals (including horses and man) or amphibians, first piercing the skin with strong jaws. Collecting for medicinal purposes (this is the leech used in the past for blood-letting) and scientific study has reduced its numbers almost to extinction so it is now very rare in the wild. Leeches are an important source of several pharmaceutical

x 1.5

compounds, especially *hirudin*, an anti-coagulant which the leech uses to prevent the blood clotting whilst it is feeding. Medicinal leeches are now being raised commercially to obtain this medically valuable substance.

FLATWORMS

Flatworms are charming little creatures with flat, soft, fragile bodies, ranging in colour from white to grey, brown or black. They have a definite head (**3b**) with dark eyespots, which are a simple form of eye, but the mouth is a protrusible tube beneath the *middle* of the body (**3a**). They move by gliding smoothly over a surface, fitting their bodies to its contours, sometimes accelerating with wriggling undulations. They cannot swim but make desperate attempts to do so if dropped into open water.

Flatworms are very common animals found crawling over mud bottoms, amongst debris (especially dead leaves), under stones or amongst vegetation.

3a

3b

Most of them feed on decomposing matter but the large *Dendrocoelum* is a hunter specialising in trapping the water louse *Asellus* in strands of sticky mucus exuded from special glands and sucking out its soft parts with the tubular mouth.

Some flatworms can reproduce by breaking pieces off from their bodies to grow into new worms. They all make spherical egg cases of hornlike material, up to 3mm in diameter, and yellowish at first but darkening to brown or black within a day or two. These are glued to solid objects mostly in the autumn. All the flatworms described here possess one pair of eyes (occasional freaks have one or two more) except for *Polycelis* which has dozens.

There are many other smaller species (not all flat) which can be very common seasonally. Most are whitish, others colourless, blackish or bright green; some form chains by joining head to tail. If a netful of debris is left to settle in a bucket of water many of these little worms may appear, crawling beneath the surface film.

Dendrocoelum (**1**) is very easy to identify because of its white or greyish colour and large size, up to 25mm. The body is very sticky and difficult to handle without damaging the animal.

Planaria (**2**) is smaller then *Dendrocoelum*, 10-12mm, and greyish-brown, with the front of its head abruptly blunted. It is rather local and less common than others mentioned here.

Dugesia includes several species. **D. polychroa** (**4**) and **D. lugubris** (**3**) are native to Europe, dark grey-brown with a rounded triangular head, both about 20mm long; *polychroa* is definitely paler beneath but *lugubris* is similar in tone above and below. A third species **D. tigrina** (**5**), introduced from North America – probably with waterplants, has become fairly common and widespread. It is up to 15mm long with a sharply triangular head and mottled coloring.

Polycelis (**6**) has numerous tiny eyespots (not easy to see without a lens) around the front half of its body, which is blackish-brown and about 15mm long.

Mesostoma (**7**) is a distinctive worm, transparent amber and firmer in texture than other flatworms. Several species ranging from 5-15mm may be found.

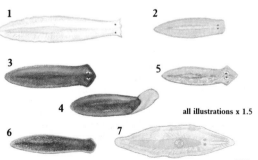

all illustrations x 1.5

HYDRAS (Cnidaria)

Hydras are the simplest of active animals and their discovery aroused great excitement amongst early scientists as they seemed to be a 'missing link' between plants and animals. However, despite their plant-like appearance they are genuine animals that feed on other creatures and move around.

The hydra's body is very elastic and contractile, especially the tentacles. Food animals, such as water fleas, are captured by the microscopic stinging cells on the tentacles and drawn in to the mouth sited between their bases. Hydras usually stay in one place, attached by the foot, but they can let go and move around by 'looping' or simply by floating off to somewhere else. Hydras are good subjects for aquaria and can be fed on water fleas; well fed specimens may bud off baby hydras from the body wall (**a**).

Green Hydra *Hydra viridis* (**2**), usually about 5mm long, is the most plantlike because it is green, due to microscopic algae within its body. It prefers clean clear waters such as spring ponds or gravel bottomed pools where it is usually attached to plants.

Brown Hydra *H. oligactis* (**1**) and others, are larger and more widespread than the Green and may become very abundant. Their bodies are up to 10mm long and the tentacles, if allowed time and space to relax, can stretch out to 100mm! But they are usually kept shorter.

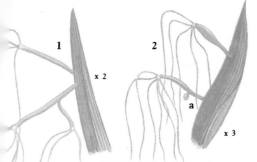

1 x 2

2

a

x 3

SPONGES (Porifera)

Sponges are simple animals consisting of an irregular, fragile, spongy-textured mass fixed to some solid object – masonry, sunken branches, wooden piles, rarely to plants. The sponge 'body' is riddled with a network of tiny tunnels through which water is drawn to provide oxygen and food, in the form of microscopic plankton.

The colour and shape of sponges depends upon where they grow. They may form a thick or thin crust, or develop into long 'fingers' reaching out into the water. In good light, sponges are green, because of microscopic algae present in the body which provide nourishment, but in gloomy conditions the green fades to yellowish as the algae die.

During autumn, tiny spheres about 1mm across appear in the base of the sponge. these are *gemmules* which survive through the cold of winter, when the sponge body disintegrates. The warmth of spring stimulates the gemmules to start growing into new sponges.

Sponge species cannot be identified without microscopic study: the commonest is **Ephydatia fluviatilis**, (**1**).

1

PROTOZOA

These are microscopic animals present in great numbers in any pond. Normally they cannot be seen with the naked eye but a few species form colonies of sufficient size to arouse the curiosity of the intelligent observer.

Bell Animals, *Vorticella* (**2**) and its allies, are tiny bell-shaped creatures on long stalks (about 1mm) which coil up like springs when contracted. Colonies form whitish halos of fuzzy speckles surrounding plants, twigs and other solid objects, even snails and crustaceans. They are common and easy to spot but if disturbed they contract and seem to disappear. The best way to study them is to put the colony, on its support, into a clear container of water, allow it time to settle and expand, then use a magnifying glass.

2

x 4

Ophrydium (**3**) forms blobs of soft clear jelly, usually about 5-10mm across but often larger. The animals themselves are tiny, bright green and form a dense stippling over the surface of the jelly. This species could easily be mistaken for an alga.

3

x 4

Terms used for plant leaves

oval   lanceolate   lobed

strap-like

LEAF EDGES

entire   toothed

serrated

leaves alternate

opposite pair

whorl

pinnate   twice-pinnate   finely divided

Index
of common and generic names

Abramis 158
Acilius 158
Acrocephalus 193
Acroloxus 216
Aedes 106
Aeshna 93
Agabus 194
Agile Frog 81
Alcedo 63
Alder 23
Alderfly 101, larva 182
Algae 136
Alisma 38
Alnus 23
Alpine Newt 79, 141
Alytes 84
Amber Snail 108
American Mink 57
Amphibians 76-85, 138-143
Amphibious Bistort 49
Anabolia 101
Anas 66-8
Anax 91
Ancylus 216
Anglers' Curse 88, nymphs 174
Anguilla 148
Anodonta 219
Anopheles 105, larva 187
Apium 40
Aplexa 214
Apus 73
Ardea 63
Argulus 206
Argyroneta 200
Arrowhead 39
Arvicola 54
Asellus 207
Astacus 208
Athripsodes 101, 184
Austropotamobius 208
Aythya 68-9

Awlwort 133
Azolla 113

Backswimmers 180
Beaver, European 53
Beetles 103, 111, 189-99
Bell Animals 233
Berula 40
Bithynia 211
Biting Midges 106, larva 188
Bitterling 162
Black Basses 168
Black-tailed Skimmer 94
Bladderworts 124
Blicca 159
Blinks 130
Blue-green Algae 136
Bloodworms 186
Bog Asphodel 51
Bogbean 51
Bog Moss 135
Bombina 84
Branta 65
Breams 158
Brown Rat 54
Brown Trout 146
Bucephala 69
Bufo 83, 142, tadpoles 142-3
Bugs 110
Bullhead, American 165
Bulrush 29
Bulrush Wainscot Moth 99
Burr-reeds 36
Butomus 37
Buttercups 50

Caddis Flies 100, larvae 182
Caenis 88, 174
Callitriche 131
Caltha 50
Canada Goose 65

235

Canary Grass 27
Carex 29-31
Carassius 155
Carps 152
Cataclysta 185
Caterpillars 185
Castor 53
Catfishes 164
Ceratophyllum 128-9
Chaetophora 137
Chara 129
Chaoborus 187
Chaser Dragonflies 94
China-mark Moth 185, larva 185
Chirocephalus 205
Chloeon 88, nymph 173
Cinclidotus 134
Cladium 32
Cladophora 137
Claret Dun 89, nymph 174
Club-rush 29
Cockle, Freshwater 220
Coenagrion 98
Colymbetes 193
Common Frog 81, tadpoles 143
Common toad 83, 142, tadpoles 143
Coot 60
Corixa 181
Cotton Grass 32
Coypu 53
Crangonyx 204
Crane Fly 107, larva 188
Crayfish 208
Crucian Carp 155
Crustacea 202-8
Crystalwort 113
Culex 106, larvae 187
Culicoides 188
Cyclops 203
Cygnus 64
Cymatia 181
Cyprinus 152

Dabchick 59
Dactylorhiza 51
Daddy-long-legs 107
Damselflies 96, nymphs 177

Daphnia 202
Daphnia 202
Darter Dragonflies 95
Delichon 73
Dendrocoelum 228
Diaptomus 203
Diving Beetles 191-5
Dolomedes 111
Donacia 103, larva 199
Dragonflies 90-5, nymphs 175-7
Dreissena 217
Drepanocladus 135
Ducks 66-9
Duckweeds 112-3
Dugesia 229
Dytiscus 191-2

Edible Frog 82, tadpole 143
Eel 148
Eiseniella 221
Eleocharis 32
Elodea 122
Emberiza 70
Emperor Dragonfly 91
Emys 75
Enallagma 98
Enteromorpha 137
Ephemera 89, nymphs 174
Ephydatia 232
Equisetum 52
Eriophorum 32
Erpodella 225
Erythromma 97
Esox 150
European Pond Terrapin 75

Fairy Shrimp 205
Filamentous algae 136
Fire Salamander 79, 141
Fish Leech 223
Fish Louse 206
Fishes 144-172
Flatworms 227-9
Fleas 202-3
Flowering Rush 37
Fontinalis 134
Fool's Water-cress 40

Frogbit 115
Frogs 80-2, tadpoles 112-3
Fulica 60

Gadwall 67
Gallinula 60
Gammarus 204
Gasterosteus 171
Gerris 111
Gipsywort 45
Glossiphonia 225
Glyceria 27
Glyphotaelius 100, larva 183
Gnats 105
Gobio 157
Goldfish 155
Golden Orfe 155
Golden Tench 156
Goldeneye 69
Goosander 69
Goose, Canada 65
Graptodytes 195
Grass Snake 74
Grasses 27
Great Crested Newt 76, 139
Grebes 58
Great Diving Beetle 191
Great Silver Beetle 197
Greendrake 89, nymph 174
Groenlandia 121
Gudgeon 157
Gut Weed 137
Gyrinus 111, 189

Haemopis 226
Halesus 101
Haliplus 190
Hawker Dragonflies 91-2
Helobdella 225
Helochares 198
Helodidae larvae 199
Helophorus 198
Hemiclepsis 224
Heron 62
Hippuris 123
Hirudo 226
Hirundo 72

Hog Louse 207
Horned Pout 165
Hornwort 128
Horse Flies 107, larva 188
Horse Leech 226
Horsetails 52
Hottonia 123
House Martin 73
Hoverfly 107
Hydra 230
Hydrobius 197
Hydrocharis 115
Hydrometra 110
Hydrophilus 196
Hydroporus 194
Hygrobia 190
Hygrotus 195
Hyla 85
Hyphydrus 195

Ictalurus 165
Ilybius 193
Ilyocoris 179
Iris 37
Iris 37
Ischnura 97
Isoetes 133
Isotomurus 109

Juncus 34

Kingcup 50
Kingfisher 63

Laccobius 198
Lagarosiphon 122
Leaf Beetle 103, larva 199
Leeches 222
Lemna 112-3
Lepomis 169
Leptocerus 101, larvae 184
Leptodictyon 135
Leptophlebia 89, nymph 174
Lestes 96
Leuciscus 155
Libellula 94
Lice 206-7

Limnephilus 101, larvae 184
Limpets 216
Littorella 132
Loach, Pond 163
Lobelia 133
Loosestrifes 45
Lutra 56
Lycopus 45
Lymnaea 212-3
Lysimachia 45
Lythrum 45

Mallard 66
Marbled Newt 77, 139
Mare's-tail 123
Marsh Frog 82
Marsh Marigold 50
Marsh Orchids 51
Mayflies 88, nymphs 173-4
Medicinal Leech 226
Mentha 47
Menyanthes 51
Mergus 69
Mesostoma 229
Micropterus 168-9
Midwife Toad 84, tadpole 143
Misgurnus 163
Mites 200
Molanna 101, larva 184
Molluscs 209-20
Montia 131
Moor Frog 80
Moorhen 60
Mosquitos 105, larvae 187
Mosses 134
Moths 98
Mud Worms 222
Muskrat 53
Mussels 216-20
Mustela 57
Mute Swan 64
Myocastor 53
Myosotis 47
Myriophyllum 126-7
Mystacides 101, larva 184

Narthecium 51
Natrix 74

Natterjack Toad 83
Neomys 53
Nepa 179
Nerite 210
Newts 76, 138
Nine-spined Stickleback 172
Nitella 129
Nonagria 99
Noterus 191
Notonecta 180
Nuphar 114
Nutria 53
Nymphaea 114
Nymphoides 115
Nymphula 98, larva 185

Oecetis 100
Oenanthe 43
Ondantra 53
Ophrydium 233
Orthetrum 94
Osiers 25
Otter 56

Pacifastacus 208
Palmate Newt 78, 140
Parsley Frog 85, tadpole 140
Paraponyx 185
Pelobates 85
Pelodytes 85
Perca 166
Perch 166
Phalaris 27
Phantom larvae 187
Phragmites 27
Phryganea 101, larvae 183
Physa 213
Pike 150
Pike-perch 167
Pintail 68
Piscicola 223
Pisidium 220
Planaria 228
Planorbarius 214
Planorbis 214-5
Plea 181
Plumed Gnats 104, larvae 186

Pochard 69
Podiceps 59
Podura 109
Polycelis 229
Polycentropus 184
Polygonum 49
Pond Loach 163
Pond Olive 88, nymph, 173
Pond Snails 212
Pond Terrapin 75
Pondweeds 118
Pool Frog 82
Potamogeton 118-21
Potamopyrgus 211
Protozoa 232
Pumpkinseed Sunfish 169
Pungitius 172
Pyrrhosoma 97

Quillworts 133

Raft Spider 111
Rallus 61
Rainbow Trout 147
Ramshorn Snails 214
Rana 80-2
Ranatra 179
Ranunculus 50, 117
Rattus 54
Reed Bunting 70
Reed Warbler 70
Reedmace 29
Reeds 27
Rhodeus 162
Riccia 113
Riparia 73
River Snails 210
Roach 161
Rorippa 48
Rudd 160
Rumex 49
Rushes 34
Rutilus 161

Sagittaria 38
Salamandra 79, 141
Salix 24-5

Sallow 24
Salmo 146-7
Sand Martin 73
Saucer Bug 179
Scardinius 160
Schoenoplectus 29
Sedge Flies 100
Sedges (Grasses) 29
Seed Shrimps 206
Segmentina 215
Shoreweed 132
Shoveler 68
Shrimps 204
Sialis 101, larva 182
Silurus 164
Sisyra 101, larva 182
Sium 40
Smooth Newt 78, 140
Snails 109
Spadefoot Toad 85, tadpole 143
Sparganium 36
Sparganophilus 221
Spearwort 50
Speedwells 46
Sphaerium 220
Sphagnum 135
Spiders 111, 200
Spike Rushes 32
Spirodela 112
Spirogyra 137
Spongefly 102, larva 182
Sponges 231
Springtails 109
Square-tailed Worm 221
Squeak Beetle 190
Stachys 45
Starworts 130
Sticklebacks 170-2
Stizostedion 167
Stoneworts 129
Stratiotes 39
Subularia 133
Succinea 108
Sunfishes 168
Sympetrum 95
Swallow 72
Swan Mussel 219

Swan 64
Sweet-grasses 27
Swift 73

Tabanus larva 188
Tachybaptus 59
Teal 67
Tench 156
Terrapin 75
Theobaldia 105
Theodoxus 210
Theromyzon 224
Tinca 156
Tipula larva 188
Toads 83-5, 172, tadpoles 143
Tree Frog 85, tadpole 143
Triaenodes 101, larvae 184
Triturus 76-79, 139-141
Troglodytes 71
Trout 146
True-Flies 104, larvae 186
Tubifex 222
Tufted Duck 68
Typha 29

Unio 219
Utricularia 124-5

Valvata 211
Valve Snails 211
Velia 110
Veronica 46
Viviparus 210
Vorticella 233

Water Beetles 189-99
Water Bloom 137
Water Boatmen 180-1
Water Celery, *see* Water Parsnips
Water Cress 48
Water Cricket 110
Water Crowfoots 116-7
Water-dock 49
Water-dropworts 43

Water Fern 113
Water Fleas 202
Water Forget-me-not 47
Waterhen 47
Water Lilies 114
Water Lobelia 133
Water Louse 207
Water Measurer 110
Water Milfoils 126
Water Mint 47
Water Mites 200
Water-parsnips 40
Water-plantains 38
Water Pepper 49
Water Rail 61
Water Rat 54
Water Scorpion 179
Water Shrew 53
Water Skater 111
Water Slater 207
Water Soldier 39
Water Speedwell 46
Water Spider 200
Water Stick-insect 179
Water Thyme 122
Water Violet 123
Water Vole 54
Weatherfish 163
Wels 164
Whirligig Beetle 111, 189, larva 189
Wigeon 67
Willow Moss 134
Willows 24, 25
Wolfia 113
Woundwort, Marsh 45
Wren 71

Yellow-bellied Toad 84
Yellow-cress 48

Zander 167
Zebra Mussel 217
Zonitoides 108